# Using Social Theory in Educational Research

*Using Social Theory in Educational Research* explores the challenges and implications of social theories within educational research. Although concepts from social theories have become commonplace within educational research over the last several decades, little attention has been paid to the challenges and opportunities these present and the problems beginning educational researchers may encounter when using such concepts in their work. This breakthrough book is organized to help practicing educators and novice researchers who have little familiarity with social theory through:

- introducing the major schools of social theory, their basic concepts and applicability to educational concepts;
- developing the researcher's understanding of the potential of social theory to improve their own practice;
- explaining how to analyze findings in the light of social theories, using practical examples and a fictional researcher;
- discussing how their work might contribute to the refinement of theories and knowledge about educational phenomena.

Accessible and illustrated with examples, *Using Social Theory in Educational Research* is essential reading for graduate students of education and educational researchers with a limited background in social theory. Experienced researchers will also find the discussion on the changes in the nature of educational research and practice over the last two decades and arguments about the usefulness of social theory within educational research provocative.

**Mark Dressman** is Associate Professor in the Department of Curriculum and Instruction at the University of Illinois at Urbana-Champaign, USA.

# Using Social Theory in Educational Research

## A practical guide

Mark Dressman

Routledge
Taylor & Francis Group

NEW YORK AND LONDON

First published 2008
by Routledge
2 Park Square, Milton Park, Abingdon, Oxon, OX14 4RN

Simultaneously published in the USA and Canada
by Routledge
270 Madison Ave, New York, NY 10016

*Routledge is an imprint of the Taylor & Francis Group, an informa business*

© 2008 Mark Dressman

Typeset in Garamond by Keyword Group Ltd
Printed and bound in Great Britain by TJ International Ltd,
Padstow, Cornwall

*British Library Cataloguing in Publication Data*
A catalog record for this book is available from the British Library

*Library of Congress Cataloging in Publication Data*
A catalog record for this book has been requested

ISBN 13: 978-0-415-43640-3 (hbk)
ISBN 13: 978-0-415-43641-0 (pbk)

ISBN 10: 0-415-43640-0 (hbk)
ISBN 10: 0-415-43641-9 (pbk)

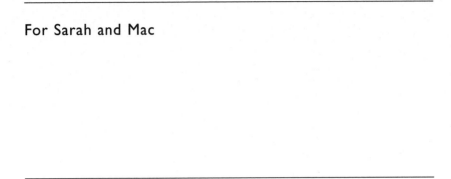

For Sarah and Mac

# Contents

# Acknowledgments

No one ever writes a book alone. In this case, I owe an enormous debt of gratitude to my colleague and good friend Fazal Rizvi, without whose support and advice in its early stages this book would never have come to be written or published. Fazal was also very instrumental in the development of the background of fictional character Rick Chavez and his class, and provided invaluable support and advice about the social and cultural milieu in which Rick and his students worked. I am also very grateful for the advice of my colleague and good friend Fouad Abd El-Khalick, who lent his expertise as a writer and in the history and philosophy of science to early drafts of chapters, and helped my arguments to stay on course.

My wife, Sarah, and son, Mac, remained in remarkably good humor during the year in which the book was written, and were very generous in allowing me the space and time to write. This book owes everything to their encouragement.

Finally, during the time that I was planning and writing the book, a doctoral student, Steve Rutledge, conducted and wrote his dissertation study, in which he followed the experiences of a journalism teacher and his students as they shot and edited a news video of events at their school. Neither Steve nor the journalism teacher is Rick Chavez, nor are the students in Steve's excellent dissertation, the events that Steve relates, or his analysis and conclusions the same as those appearing in Chapters Three and Four of this book. However, the general premise of Steve's study and the general course of his research were the inspiration for the portrait of Rick Chavez and his research project. Steve was also gracious to read a draft of Chapter Three and to provide detailed and very useful feedback. I am very grateful to Steve Rutledge and acknowledge the contribution that his fine work made to my imagination.

# Introduction
## The power of social theory
## for educational research

> An ant writing for other ants, this fits my project very well!
> (Bruno Latour, *Reassembling the Social* 2005: 9)

## Introduction

On the edge of a city in the early years of this new century, a group of teachers sit with their building administrator and try to account for scores from their school's most recent round of state-mandated exams. The administrator distributes scores for the students in each class to individual teachers and in her remarks focuses on comparative gains or losses from previous years across subject areas or subgroups of students, such as males and females or groups disaggregated for their national origin, race, and indicators of family background and income. She asks questions she hopes will get the teachers to share ideas about how to raise scores in the next round. What accounts for incidents of increase? Was it a new textbook? Greater alignment of instruction with test content? A new instructional approach? And what might explain declines in some classes? What do the teachers think they can do to make sure the declines are reversed next year and the gains remain?

But most of the teachers are having none of it. When pressed to explain why her students' scores improved over the previous year, one teacher says she had a "really good group this year" with "no problem students." When pressed to explain declines, other teachers allude to problematic encounters with parents or to their students' lack of preparedness at the beginning of the school year. A few bring up individual cases of students to illustrate these points and note how consistent their performance has been across areas tested.

The meeting ends in frustration for all, with the administrator irritated that the teachers are not more results oriented, and the teachers more determined than ever not to hold themselves accountable for the educational consequences of what they believe are due to forces beyond their control. Afterwards, they gather in small groups to discuss what they believe are "the real issues." One teacher remembers how it used to be back before "all these foreign students" arrived, and back "when families had two parents" and when you called a student's home in the evenings "and an adult answered the phone." Another teacher bemoans the exams, which she says "dumb-down and trivialize what it means to learn." But a third teacher disagrees. In his view, "It's always been his way—a few kids want to do well in school because they see they'll get ahead. The rest, well, school's there for the basics and to watch the kids while the parents work. It's just the way things are." And nearly all agree that the easier gratifications of the Internet, video games, and other media are a growing part of the problem. One cites a story on a recent television news program in which a teenager's "addiction" to online gaming caused him to become withdrawn and fail in school until his family and teachers intervened.

This fictional scenario, which is a composite of my own experiences and stories of similar incidents told by colleagues, is representative of the tensions and challenges that face educators in many industrialized and industrializing societies today. Across the globe, citizens and their governments have embraced, with little if any reservation, the proposition that ever-greater levels of educational achievement are key to producing ever-greater levels of economic prosperity and social well-being for individuals, their families, communities, and nations. And although the details of this scenario may vary from school to school, from region to region, or from primary to secondary to postsecondary levels, the assumptions that warrant policies and that are embodied in the words and deeds of teachers, students, parents, and administrators remain remarkably similar.

Just as consistent is that almost everywhere, mass education is perceived as fraught with problems. In industrialized nations, educators and policy makers struggle to make mass education more equitable and successful for students from increasingly diverse religious, cultural, linguistic, and economic backgrounds. Throughout the industrializing world, from Mexico to India, parents who can afford it send their children to private schools, where classes are smaller, teachers are more accountable, and the curriculum is geared to preparing students for professional careers. Everywhere, from Morocco, where a massive restructuring and realignment of primary, secondary, and higher education is underway, to the USA, where a recent cover article in *Time* magazine chided policy makers for "aiming too low" in their focus on raising reading and math scores (Wallis *et al.* 2006), the g-word, *globalization*, is on the lips of pundits and politicians. And yet, whenever teachers and administrators around the world gather to discuss practical responses to these issues, the tenor of their discussion typically echoes that of my introductory scenario.

## Purpose of the book

This book is written for individuals interested in moving beyond the stalemate that characterizes much discussion about how to "fix" mass education today. Its aim is to provide an introduction to an alternative and more formally developed group of theories about the social world, and to outline a set of practices whereby educators and researchers might use social theories to generate fresh insights about educational problems. The book builds on a growing body of research that is framed by multiple schools of social theory, and responds to sea changes in the nature of educational research and its practice that have taken place over the last two decades. Prior to 1990, educational research was overwhelmingly the province of advanced doctoral and postdoctoral studies, and theories were typically closely grounded in experimentally collected evidence and used to generate hypotheses, which were then tested using quantitative methods of measurement and analysis. Beginning in the 1980s, however, educational phenomena were increasingly viewed as the product of historical, economic, and sociocultural forces that produced behaviors that were too subtle and complex in their dynamics to be experimentally manipulated and quantified. The rise of a broad range of theories based on linguistic and Marxist-influenced theories in Europe and of sociolinguistic theory in the USA also contributed to changes in the nature of the questions researchers asked and the methods they used to investigate them. At the same time, movements in the professionalization of teaching urged teachers to exercise their own initiative, or agency, in finding answers to educational problems through informal, typically qualitative practices known as action, or teacher research.

As research methodology has broadened in its scope, the ways in which theories are used have changed as well, from the generation of hypotheses to be tested to the use of theories as rhetorical "framing" devices that provide powerful metaphors that in some cases organized entire research projects. Surprisingly little, however, has been written about this change in the use of theory and its implications for researchers' practices, especially for how social theory supports, or warrants, the arguments researchers make in their writings. A second purpose of this book, then, is to outline the multiple ways that social theory is currently used in educational research and to examine the implications of its use for educational research, for policy making, and for educational practice.

## What is social theory?

As I use the term in this book, *social theory* describes a broad range of philosophical, economic, historical, linguistic, social–psychological, and literary arguments generated by Western scholars in the nineteenth and twentieth centuries in response to the period of social history known as *modernity*. Modernity, in this sense, refers to a period of great social, technological, and political change in the Western world that began in the seventeenth century and became a fully established philosophical and scientific movement known as the Enlightenment in the eighteenth century. With the full development of industrial capitalism and mass institutions such as public schools and universities, hospitals, prisons, libraries, and museums in the nineteenth century and consumer capitalism and electronic mass media in the twentieth century—but also mass warfare, mass genocide, and nuclear weaponry—by the end of the last century, modernity seemed to many philosophers and social theorists to have run amok, or by others simply to have run its course.

The logic of modernity, or modernism, is the perspective and set of assumptions about reality that most of the westernized world takes for granted today. For example, modernism holds that as *individuals* and not as members of any privileged class, race, or religious group, we all have the right to life and an equitable share of what our world offers (e.g. to be paid a living wage; to live and travel where we wish; to be educated and have access to health care; to participate in government); that it makes sense to divide the people of the world into nations based on cultural and geographic contiguity, and for these nations to have control over their internal affairs; and that science and technology bring truth and progress. Most important, rationality—the capacity of human beings to think through and solve problems based on objective evidence that has been freed from the assumed emotionality and superstition of the premodern world—is held to be the primary source of all of modernity's gifts. And if, as is also evident, great inequities remain within the social order of nations, genocide periodically rages, countries still go to war, and science and technology have also brought us global warming and weapons of mass destruction that were unimaginable in earlier epochs, we do not conclude that these conditions persist because modernism is itself somehow flawed. Instead, we assume it is because the world remains in transition and modernism's promise has yet to be realized.

But here's the catch, and the point from which nearly all social theory that offers a critique of modernity departs: It is that any social vision so seductive that it essentially blocks out our ability to imagine the universe otherwise or that excuses current atrocities as bumps on the road to a better future cannot be one that is fully rational, either in its origins or its plan. Ironically, the more tightly that categories and strictures of objectivity are applied within social and political realms, the more dehumanizing outcomes may become. In the last century, it was rationality that justified apartheid as a "solution" to racial difference in South Africa, for example, and the rationalized need for an objectively "purer" and "more normative" population that led Nazi Germany to round up not only Jews but homosexuals, the Roma, and the physically and mentally disabled, and send them to concentration camps, "for their own good" as well as the good of the nation.

Social theory's potential to provide educators and educational researchers with a source of insight into social and educational problems extends far beyond a critical historical account of modernity and the consequences of rationalism, however. Indeed, to gather as wide a range of independently developed and revised philosophical, historical, economic, literary, and linguistic arguments as I refer to here under the umbrella of a single term may be to misname them. Social theory, as I use it in this book and as it is currently applied within educational research, is not one thing. It is, rather, a loose collection of extremely diverse perspectives with multiple origins, each of which addresses the logic of modernity in a unique way.

These qualities of social theory—its critique of the institutions and social order of modernity, the diversity and creativity of its multiple perspectives, and its argumentative, or *agonistic*, modus operandi—make it a powerful research tool within educational contexts. To illustrate the range of social theory's potential and to introduce a second line of discussion in this book about some of the limitations and problems associated with the ways it is currently applied in educational research, I turn to a brief review of studies that have made use of diverse schools of social theory.

## Applying social theory: some examples

The simplest and most direct use of social theory within research may occur when a single word or phrase from theory is applied as a descriptor to an educational phenomenon. For example, although the word *discourse* has a meaning similar to that of the word *conversation* in its common usage, Aziz Talbani (1996) borrowed a more specific, Foucauldian (Foucault 1980) use of *discourse* to describe the cultural process of Islamization in modern Pakistan whereby

> Societal discourse mediates its power and control through institutions and elites who 'are charged with saying what counts as true' (Foucault 1980: 131). A regime uses political, economic, and social apparatuses to control and dominate. Truth is established through the discourse of power that is related, preserved, and legitimized. (Talbani 1996: 67)

Talbani opened his research essay with a short discussion of the Foucauldian implications of discourse for establishing what counts as truth and as knowledge within a given society and time period. He characterized the Qur'an in fundamentalist Islamic societies as the discursively authorized "core of knowledge" (Talbani 1996: 67), and continued his analysis with an historical description of scholarship in the Islamic world from the eighth century to the modern history of Pakistan, noting changes in discursive regimes of truth over thirteen centuries. Within the text of the article, the term *discourse* was described in detail at the beginning of the article and was used throughout its body and concluding paragraphs, but its theoretical implications were not discussed beyond the article's introduction.

A slightly broader use of a social theoretical concept in the design of an empirical, classroom-based study was made by two Dutch researchers, Paul Leseman and Peter de Jong (1998), who used a theoretical framework "based on neo-Piagetian and neo-Vygotskian theorizing" and borrowed the term *apprenticeship* to characterize "assume(d) ... opportunities for literacy-related activities and... processes of appropriation of knowledge, skills, and values involved in these practices through socially arranged forms of participation" (Leseman and de Jong 1998: 33) in the homes of young children of multiple national and religious backgrounds in The Netherlands. As in the case of the article by Talbani, this article began with a theoretical discussion of the special meaning of a common term. Unlike Talbani, however, Leseman and de Jong's theoretical framework and its assumptions about the existence and extent of home literacy practices formed the premise for the study as well as its analytical categories, rather than simply serving as a descriptor applied to a set of pre-existing historical events.

An example of an even more extensive use of social theory is provided by a comparative study of science education across elementary, secondary, and university classrooms by two Finnish researchers, Sinikka Kaartinen and Kristiina Kumpulainen (2001), which used a school of social theory grounded in the work of Soviet-era psychologist Lev Vygotsky and later sociocultural theorists and researchers. As in the previous examples, a discussion of the study's theoretical background and a review of previous research prefaced the report of methods and findings. However, this discussion moved beyond the appropriation of terminology or use of theory as a premise for an empirical investigation into the realm of advocacy for a vision of science instruction that sociocultural learning theory and previous research supported: "[T]he social practices constructed in these (sociocultural) learning situations have the potential to support meaningful and student-sensitive learning, in contrast to routinized and mechanistic procedures" (Kaartinen and Kumpalainen 2001: 4). Beyond the introduction and discussion of analytical categories, the report of each finding of the study was referenced directly back to sociocultural theory, and the Discussion and Conclusion section focused on substantiating and aligning findings very positively with theory: "Here, the students can be characterized as architects of their own learning as they actively design, carry out and reflect on the nature of their activity." Social theory in this report was not used simply as a source of terms or as the study's premise, but as an ideological scaffold that both supported and was supported by the researchers' theoretical argument.

Or, consider the analysis of British researcher Nell Keddie (1971), who studied the ways in which teachers justified the streaming, or tracking, of secondary students based on their ratings of individual students' intelligence, motivation, and initiative, which also correlated highly with social class: Students rated in the A group were nearly always middle class, B students were from lower middle class homes, and C students were almost inevitably working class. Her description of the process was discursively reproductive of the social order, in which teachers' comments not only about, but to, students were received by the students differently, according to the experience of their social class background:

> A stream students have been told, and they told me, that learning to work independently (of teacher and textbook) will help them 'in the sixth form and at university.' I also heard a teacher telling a B group that 'any worker who can think for himself is worth his weight in gold to his employer.' It is likely that lower stream pupils know this to be a highly questionable statement and do not look forward to this kind of satisfaction from their work. (Keddie 1971: 138)

As in the example of the study of science education in Finland by Kaartinen and Kumpulainen, social theory in the work of Keddie and other British researchers in the 1970s functioned as a kind of all-encompassing architecture for the analysis and interpretation of findings, but with a crucial difference. Whereas sociocultural learning theory articulated and advocated an alternative vision of classroom reality in the case of science education, in the studies by Keddie and others it articulated a vision of the social world so deterministic and so completely focused on the Marxist dictum that the ultimate achievement of capitalist societies is the reproduction of the means of production that no alternate interpretation was possible: A world so perfectly, so rationally and yet so ironically constructed that every institution and every social gesture or remark could/must be seen to curve inward toward the reproduction of an over- (and pre-) determined social outcome.

But consider, as a final set of examples, a study of social constructivism conducted in a middle school social studies classroom by Margaret Sheehy (2002) and a comparison of humanities education in England and France by

Michalina Vaughan and Jane Mark-Lawson (1986). In the Vaughan and Mark-Lawson study, changes in the humanities curriculum in English and French secondary schools during the twentieth century were compared using a theory of educational stratification and social and cultural reproduction developed by French sociologists and social theorists Pierre Bourdieu and Jean-Claude Passeron (1977). In their analysis, they found that while Bourdieu's account of relations between cultural values and social status explained shifts in French curriculum policy, differences in the overall status and power of teachers had significantly altered these relations in the English context in ways that did not align with the work of Bourdieu and Passeron. They concluded, "Our comparison between France and England, while not directly challenging Bourdieu's notion of cultural capital, suggests that his tendency to generalize about Western education from French evidence is invalid" (Vaughan and Mark-Lawson 1986: 146).

Similarly, Margaret Sheehy described the struggle that she and her co-teacher, Jade, faced when they attempted to interrupt the standard curriculum of a middle school in the United States by teaching a "constructivist," interdisciplinary unit in which students were to design a new school building for themselves. In her account, Sheehy imagined that, as her reading of constructivism had promised, the opportunity to break free from the confines of traditional school tasks would produce a new social order within the classroom that would also lead to the creation of new genres and interdisciplinary understanding. But this largely did not occur. Confused by the lack of clear disciplinary and genre-based rules, the students at times did not engage in productive activities in the ways the teachers hoped. These events led Sheehy to challenge the capacity of constructivism, which in her and Popkewitz's (1998) analysis conceives of curricular change as something that can take place in classrooms independent of larger historical and macrosocial forces, to have any lasting or productive effect on schooling:

> Jade and I had acted outside history. We made the mistake constructivists make when we underestimated the full force of curricular relations that extend beyond the classroom in unfathomable ways and are not yet understood by researchers but definitely felt by teachers. (Sheehy 2002: 302)

In these two cases, social theory played as significant a role in the design of the study and analysis of findings as it did in Talbani's analysis of the Islamization of education in Pakistan or in the use of sociocultural learning theory in the cross-age study of science education by Kaartinen and Kumpulainen. However, in these latter cases, social theory did not align positively with findings from the studies. Instead, in the case of Vaughan and Mark-Lawson, differences in outcomes of curricular change in England and France challenged the generalizability of Bourdieu and Passeron's theory of social and cultural reproduction, while in the case of Sheehy, findings were used to substantiate Popkewitz's theoretical critique of constructivist theory and practice.

This brief review of studies has allowed only a limited glimpse of the scope of research topics, multiple schools of thought, and variety of uses to which social theory is applied within educational research today, but even still it is one that will likely raise many questions, if not doubts, in the minds of educators and researchers from strict empiricist traditions. It raises the question, first, of whether there are any rules to the use of social theory in educational research, or whether, as one well-known qualitative methodologist has advised, "You can be very creative when doing this sort of analysis; there is definitely no single way to perform it" (Carspecken 1996: 202). Second, the multiplicity of schools of social theory may raise questions about which school and which aspects of social theory best "fit" the educational situation under study, and at which point in an investigation social theory is best introduced. Finally, the over-determinism of a school of social theory such as Marxism/neo-Marxism, or the position of advocacy toward a particular vision of pedagogical practice that is often warranted as constructivism, raises the possibility of cases in which, rather than illuminate or contribute to the general significance of a study, an uncritical or non-circumspect use of social theory might obscure or unduly bias a researchers' analysis and conclusions.

## The rhetoric of educational research

This book begins with the assumption that there is no set of procedures— a flow-chart, if you will—that can enable educators and educational researchers to pick a social theory and use it in ways that will reliably produce findings and conclusions about educational phenomena that are objectively valid. But on the other hand, neither will it be assumed in the following chapters that the use of social theory is an entirely subjective matter, one best left up to the proclivities of individual researchers with their individual purposes or agendas. Instead, I assume that educators and educational researchers who read this book are interested in conducting research that will have an impact beyond their own understanding of a situation, that they expect to use social theory in their investigations in a way that will, either through written text or oral presentation, persuade others of the validity, both ethically and epistemologically, of their analyses and conclusions and in such a way that, ultimately, educational situations will change for the better for all parties involved. I assume, in other words, that educators and educational researchers expect that the use of social theory in their research will do some social work, and accomplish some social good.

This assumption makes the use of social theory in educational research, and the doing of educational research itself, into a *rhetorical* process. I do not mean, as the word *rhetorical* often implies in its contemporary usage, that using social theory in educational research is part of a process in which readers or listeners are somehow tricked or deceived through emotional or linguistic slights of hand into believing that an argument makes sense. Rather, I mean that, after a broad range of philosophers of language, including Wittgenstein, Toulmin, Austin and Searle, and Habermas, that whenever meaning is at stake, the use of language takes on a gaming quality, that the game is one with rules of evidence and argumentation, that the rules are known by all players, speakers/writers and listeners/readers alike, and that when the game is played honestly and openly, meaning is clarified and added to, and knowledge about social, educational phenomena, albeit limited and always incomplete, can be produced. Within a rhetorical, gaming frame of assumptions, then, questions to be asked about the use of social theory within educational research have less to do with what is objectively (or subjectively) "best" but instead with a social theory's rhetorical consequences within a research project, that is, with how potential readers or listeners who are also knowledgeable of the theory used will make sense of, and persuaded by its use within the researcher's arguments and claims.

The following chapters are designed both as an introduction to the rhetorical uses of social theory in educational research and, for experienced researchers and readers of social theory, as a more advanced text about the epistemological and methodological implications of the ways that social theory is currently used and how its use might be improved. However, the breadth and depth of perspectives within theories covered by social theory, as well as the very *ad hoc*, anti-structural, Nietzschean (Nietzsche 1955, 2006) spirit of many of social theorists and their work, presents a serious challenge to anyone wanting to describe their implications for empirical educational research. There is something about social theory, in other words, that doesn't want to be "used." Michel Foucault's (1977) very literary and lucid discussion of "the examination" in *Discipline and Control*, for instance, invites readers to meditate on the metaphor of examination and its historical implications for contemporary schooling, not to summarize the points about examination that Foucault makes and then apply them systematically to the coding of observational data collected in a school during a period of high-stakes testing. And yet this is the sort of rhetorical, analytical use to which much social theory is inevitably, and, I would argue, often unavoidably put in educational research.

How dreadful, aficionados of Theory (with a capital T) might say; how utterly crass and antithetical to Theory's postmodern mandate, to its critique of proceduralism, instrumentalism, and the linearity of objective representation. But also, I would note, how *pragmatic*, in the American philosophical sense of the word; and also, in those cases where researchers acknowledge and take into practical account the contradictions and ironies inherent in adapting abstract concepts to the study of specific, historical phenomena, and even further in those cases where the analysis of data results in the refinement and expansion of theoretical concepts, how resourceful, how generative, and how completely antithetical to the theory–practice dichotomy on which so much academic snobbery depends.

## Spirit and plan of the book

It is in the spirit and with the intent of this latter goal, to bring social theory more fully into the practice of educational research and in the process contribute to the rhetoric of social theory, that the following chapters were written. Chapter One, "Reading social theory," provides a more detailed and systematic organization to the major schools of social theory that are commonly used to frame educational research today. The chapter begins with a discussion of the difficulties inherent in reading many social theoretical texts. It moves to an introductory discussion of the central ideas of four seminal researchers and theorists of the nineteenth century, as well as a brief discussion of the influence of several other figures. The second half of the chapter provides a review of the principal major ideas of major theorists and schools of theory from the last century to the present, organized into four overlapping topics: language, discourse, meaning, and practice. The final section of the chapter provides advice on strategies for reading social theory, along with a review of helpful online resources and books.

Chapter Two, "Social theory and the rhetoric of educational research," takes up a detailed and systematic analysis of the multiple ways in which theory is currently used in educational research, both in experimental and quasi-experimental research and in observational, ethnographic, and qualitative approaches. Regardless of a researcher's method or approach to designing a study, collecting data, and analyzing and interpreting findings, two aspects of this activity are axiomatic within the chapter. The first is that data never speak for themselves, that is, that the sense that researchers make of their activities and experience is the product of presuppositions about what research is, about what is and isn't important, and about what they think the practical and theoretical implications of what they find can, will, and should be. The second axiom of educational research is that doing research is a *rhetorical* activity, that is, that the process of conducting research is part of a larger process of making arguments about some aspect of education as a phenomenon, arguments meant to persuade someone— researchers themselves, other researchers, participants, policy makers, or the public in general—that the view of educational reality that the research produces or supports is true, or valid, and that something should happen or that people should behave in a certain way as a result.

The chapter begins with a discussion of these two axioms, and is followed by an analysis of how social theory contributes in four general ways to arguments made by educational researchers, illustrated by examples from multiple studies: as foundational premise, as a focusing lens, as narrative scaffold, and as a dialectical scaffold for criticism. Concluding sections of the chapter focus on a critical discussion of the limitations of social theory's usefulness within current educational research practice.

Chapters Three and Four provide a practical illustration of the use of social theory within the context of a single project. These two chapters alternate between expository discussions of the theoretical and practical challenges to designing, conducting, and writing up research with social theory, and the fictional narrative of one teacher researcher's use of social theory in the research process. Chapter Three, "Framing research theoretically," focuses on the use of social theory in the conceptualization, design, and data collection phases of a research project. Expository discussions of these topics alternate with the story of how, step by step, a fictional secondary modern history teacher named Rick Chavez, who is interested in studying the use of digital video in his teaching, designs a study in which a group of disaffected adolescents in his class are provided a digital video camera and assigned to produce a video on the current conflicts in the Middle East and Afghanistan.

Chapter Four, "Writing with social theory," continues with the fictional case of Rick Chavez and his students described in Chapter Three. Again, narrative sections alternate with expository sections focusing on data analysis and qualitative and ethnographic writing. In the narrative, Rick Chavez draws on multiple theoretical frameworks, including theories of social and cultural reproduction, recent theory and research about adolescents' multiliteracies, and the work of global cultural theorist Arjun Appadurai (1996), to account for his students' apparent initial resistance to the video project, their formation into working groups, and the stylistic features and content of the video segments they have produced. Expository sections in the chapter focus on using social theory in reflexive, critical ways, on how to "enter the conversation" of education research through publication, and on ways of structuring and styles of writing qualitative and ethnographic research.

Chapter Five, "Social theory and the production of general educational knowledge," summarizes the major points of the book and concludes with the argument that the use of social theory can act as a network whereby individual qualitative studies can be interwoven to produce a body of ever-evolving general knowledge about educational phenomena. To illustrate and provide a summative review of the book's contents, the hypothetical case described in Chapters Three and Four as well as other published studies and other examples used as examples in the book are used as examples of how a more critical and rigorous use of both theory and related previous research would contribute to the building of general bodies of research-based knowledge about educational practices.

## Summary and conclusion

Across the globe, schools and mass education at the beginning of the twenty-first century are part-and-parcel of the same "common sense" logic that created them, a logic grounded in a passion for rationality that has seduced the imagination of Northern Europe and its extended cultural spheres for more than two centuries. This is a definitively *modern* form of logic whose normative force often conceals the full social complexity of educational situations and problems from the view of educators and educational researchers, and prevents the formulation of educational policies and pedagogical responses that will lead to improvement in educational equity and achievement. Social theories grounded in the critique of modernity and its logic offer educators and researchers a diverse set of perspectives for seeing through or "interrupting" this logic, and in many instances for projecting alternative educational practices.

However, the use of social theory as a tool of educational research is a far more complex topic than it might first appear. Social theory as I refer to it in this book is not a single thing, but rather a loose set of philosophical, historical, literary, linguistic, and economic perspectives grounded in the cultural and rhetorical traditions of their authors' own national and historical backgrounds. Moreover, social theory's uses, as illustrated through a brief review of published studies, are multiple, at times contradictory, and always open to the criticism that their adaptation to the analysis of specific educational events is a misuse that violates the spirit and intent of their authors, and that may result in their serious misinterpretation.

Consequently, educators and researchers interested in using the insights of social theory in their work are urged to revise their ideas about what research is, from the search for the "objective" truth of a phenomenon to a rhetorical activity whose goal is to produce an argument about the meaning of a phenomenon that will persuade equally or more knowledgeable others of its rightness. To this end, the beginning chapters of the book are oriented toward the explication of a rhetorical model of research and a further analysis of social theories and their usefulness in the investigation of educational phenomena, the middle chapters provide a concrete example of how social theory might inform one teacher's study of his own classroom, and the concluding chapter presents a plan for the use of social theory as an interface for the building of bodies of socially situated, general educational knowledge.

# Chapter 1

# Reading social theory

## Introduction

To the uninitiated reader, the language of contemporary social theory may often appear impenetrable, even Gordian in its construction, as though it were written to resist reading. In a legend of Ancient Greece, a knot was so elaborately and intricately tied that at first even Alexander the Great was unable to find its ends, and so a way into unraveling its complexities. But Alexander was not to be denied; he alternately raised his sword and sliced it in half, as in one account, or pulled the post out of the knot's center, causing it to fall into a loose pile of cords, as in another. Either way, destiny and Alexander's ambition became as one.

Readers of social theory are faced with an even greater challenge than that of the Gordian Knot, however, for its discourses are not composed of a single strand of thought wound round a single axis. They are, instead, composed of multiple, interwoven and quite frequently discontinuous threads wound sometimes round themselves and sometimes around multiple, branching axes with no single center. There is no simple point of release, as in the latter version of Alexander's solution, whereas to take his former approach and make a clean slice through the center would be to destroy the fabric or substance of the discourses themselves, and thus likely render them useless rather than useful to readers with the practical ambition of integrating them into their research.

This is the case not only at the conceptual level, but also at the level of writing and reading. Take, for example, this single sentence, from an early chapter of *The Logic of Practice*, by French sociologist Pierre Bourdieu:

> The conditionings associated with a particular class of conditions of existence produce *habitus*, systems of durable, transposable dispositions, structured structures predisposed to function as structuring structures, that is, as principles which generate and organize practices

and representations that can be objectively adapted to their own outcomes without presupposing a conscious aiming at ends or an express mastery of the operations necessary in order to attain them. (Bourdieu 1990: 53)

Reading this sentence without prior knowledge of Bourdieu's work, I suspect that even the most technically proficient readers would tend to lose focus just after the fourth comma, stop, refocus on the act of reading itself rather than on the meaning of the words themselves, and then notice that their comprehension was vague to almost nil. One might argue that this was a trick—that sentences lifted out of context often are unintelligible, and so the example exaggerated the effect—until, turning to the full text, a reader would soon realize that this sentence was typical of many, and that their cumulative effect was not of emerging clarity but more likely of snowballing frustration.

What accounts for, if not justifies, this complexity in the writing of many social theorists today? Is it bad translation, or perhaps a perverse desire to remain opaque and so evade cross-examination and critique, or is it actually the case that the concepts themselves are so complex that they require new forms of syntactic and semantic inventiveness? As an Anglophone reader accustomed to short sentences, common uses of vocabulary, and a rhetorical tradition in which it is incumbent on the author to explain herself in such a way that any general reader would be able to grasp the basic idea of a passage the first time through, I admit that all of the above possibilities have occurred to me more than once as I struggled through the major works of continental theorists such as Jurgen Habermas, Julia Kristeva, or Ludwig Wittgenstein, or the American pragmatist, John Dewey.

But it seems more likely that the stylistic challenges of social theory are due to a combination of two factors. The first is the academic culture in which most of these authors write, a tradition that prefers literary technique and the specialist audience over prosaic clarity and the common reader. The second, loftier reason is these authors' self-conscious rejection of, and refusal to cater to, modernism and modernist ideas about language and writing, namely, that these are shared tools for transmitting ideas from one individual's mind to other individuals' minds with little or no distortion. For these authors, the use of words with supposedly common meanings combined in deceptively simple ways is a part of the "common sense" logic of modernity that conceals more than it reveals. Writing simply to meet the needs of a broad, untutored audience is for these theorists a practice whereby meanings are not so much locked *in* as locked *up*—that is, a practice that requires an author to ignore the history of words' uses and the variations among readers and writers across history and cultures, and so truncates, or shuts down, the full transmission of meaning. Their response is to argue that communication of the sort that modernist theories of language imagine can happen is not only impossible but undesirable, and to try instead to write in such a way that the full complexity of a topic is opened up for themselves and readers with a prior knowledge of the complexity of the words and ideas they reference in their writing.

Ironically, then, the complexity of social theory's language is ultimately about producing clarity of meaning and not, as it would seem to initiates, about shutting some readers out of its discourses. In fact, the authors of social theory are not writing to initiates at all, but instead to a rather select audience who share their rhetorical disposition and, more important, their perspective on the social and intellectual history of the West over the past three centuries, and who are in general agreement about the identity of its seminal intellectual figures and the implications of those figures' work for our current social and intellectual condition.

The way into the discourses of social theory, then, is not through incisive strokes of insight or of intellectual force. Instead, understanding social theory requires the application of background knowledge of its authors' general perspective on modernism's social and intellectual history, combined with a good deal of personal resolve in the form of patience, the willingness to reread, and, so long as one compares and contrasts among multiple sources, the use of commentaries and the Internet. In this chapter I hope to fuel that resolve by providing a very basic grasp of the disposition most social theorists share toward the social and intellectual history of the past three centuries, a brief overview of social theory's main discourses and its central figures, and, in conclusion, a guide to further reading, both in hard copy text and on the Internet.

## A different view of history

The image of progress that motivates social theorists' work is grounded in an historical narrative far different from the one presented in school textbooks, the news media, and the documentary reality of The History Channel™. In those texts, scientific discoveries and new inventions are celebrated as advances in human knowledge that bring social advancements in the form of greater food yields, cures for catastrophic diseases, the spread of democracy and prosperity, and ever greater autonomy and individual freedom for the "average" citizen of an integrated "nation-state." Within this narrative, negative social consequences of technological and scientific progress, such as the routine abuse of factory workers in the nineteenth century, the development of nuclear and chemical weapons in the twentieth, or the destruction of the environment through overpopulation and pollution, are characterized as temporary setbacks and problems created out of excessive and naive enthusiasm for progress, and problems whose likely solution is the self-conscious use of ever more refined forms of technology.

The historical narrative followed by social theorists, however, parallels and at points undermines the largely positive vision presented in textbooks and the popular media. It does not celebrate inventions that changed the course of history such as the steam engine, the cotton gin, the electric light bulb, or the Internet as unproblematic landmarks in the story of modern progress. Instead, their narrative focuses on the practices, institutions, and technologies of human control that developed in response to the enormous social and cultural change wrought by the Enlightenment of the eighteenth century and the Industrial Revolution that followed. In their narrative, industrialization and the establishment of colonies brought a final end to agrarian, feudal politics and economies, as cities swelled with displaced peasants looking for work in factories. A new middle class was invented to manage expanding and increasingly complex business relations and the mass institutions—schools, hospitals, prisons, a standing military, museums, libraries—that had been created as technologies for disciplining and stabilizing the political and cultural needs and desires of a large, culturally unwashed, and potentially dangerous population of impoverished factory workers. These new institutions borrowed their structuring principles and organizational logic largely from observations of orderliness in nature, and made a virtue of all the qualities needed for the orderly management of vast numbers of people and objects within a relatively limited amount of space, such as regularity of movement, timeliness, and automaticity.

A second way that the historical narrative that motivates social theory differs from the conventional narrative of progress is in its characterization of the human condition and its response to technological innovation. There is a timelessness about humanity in the conventional narrative. Like movie stars who portray historical figures in period costume dramas but whose consciousness is clearly modern, regardless of whether they are acting the part of Rameses or Elizabeth I or Abraham Lincoln, within the conventional narrative there is a presumption that human relations, human desire, and human values are unchanging over time. Changes in people's behavior produced by technological innovations are also considered to be largely superficial, that is, having more to do with raising life expectancy and bringing convenience to people's lives than with changing how people make sense of each other and the world around them.

In contrast, social theorists largely assume that the human condition and human identities are far more malleable, and that people's material circumstances have a profound effect on the ways that they make sense of basic concepts such as time and space, as well as on how they imagine themselves as actors in the world and their relations with others. They note the extent to which historical documentation shows how a seemingly stable and timeless relationship like marriage has actually changed dramatically in response to changes in economic demands in its legal and economic meanings over time, or how practices and relations around race, sexuality, and childhood shift as economic and political circumstances change. In short, the structures and the structural logic of the institutions and spaces of modern life are seen to be structured by, and in turn to have a structuring effect on, the logic and dispositions that organize both society at large and the most personal and intimate relations of human life.

## Four seminal figures

In addition to a general, alternative view of social and intellectual history, contemporary social theory draws heavily from the work of four philosophers and social scientists of the mid- to late nineteenth century: the German economic philosopher and historian Karl Marx, the British scientist Charles Darwin, the francophone Swiss linguist Ferdinand de Saussure, and the German philosopher Friedrich Nietzsche. Before moving to the principal ideas of current theorists, I present a brief overview of the most influential ideas of these figures.

### Karl Marx

No single individual has had more influence on contemporary social theory than the German philosopher of economy, history, and social revolution, Karl Marx (Kolakowski and Falla 2005; McLellan 1988). In his lifetime, Marx witnessed and chronicled the physical, social, and psychological abuses of the industrial revolution within the population of Europe, and produced the most acidic and penetrating analysis of capitalism in history.

Marxist theory is grounded in a complicated and sometimes inaccurate reading of German philosopher Georg Wilhelm Friedrich Hegel's theory of historical progression, that today is commonly labeled (but was never named by Hegel as) a *dialectical* process. In that reading, the social, political, economic, and cultural order of one period of history produces consequences that lead to a reactive next period which attempts to compensate for excesses of the former period. But this new, corrective order is also flawed, and in time is replaced by a third order, in which the contradictions and problems of the previous two eras are largely resolved. Hegel's prime example of his triadic, three-stage description of historical process during his own lifetime was the French Revolution, a movement whose revolutionary energy but weak intellectual foundations led to the Reign of Terror, and whose excesses, once exhausted, led to the political resolution of a constitutional state composed of free citizens.

Hegel's philosophical position made him the darling of the Prussian state, which appropriated his views to legitimate its own existence as the resolution of previously flawed regimes. He had only been dead a few years when Marx entered the university in Berlin, and his philosophy remained paramount in its curriculum. But Marx and the group of students who came to be known, ironically, as the Young Hegelians, were not so enamored of the Prussian state or its orthodoxies. They were particularly critical of Hegel's characterization of the motivating force behind historical progression as *Geist,* a word often translated into English as "ghost" or "spirit," and its implication to them, either rightly or wrongly, that a divine presence, whose popular manifestation was religion, was the driving, directive force of history. Instead, Marx kept the concept of dialectic to describe historical progression, but argued that its motivating force was class struggle, that is, a persistent tension between the *haves*, or those who owned and controlled material wealth, or *capital*, and the *have nots*, or those who served the interests of those with wealth. The legitimating source of this imbalance, according to Marx, was religion and religious doctrine, which throughout history had always sided with the wealthy, and whose promises and focus on eternal reward and punishment and divine intervention in earthly affairs (such as historical progression), distracted the working classes from rising up and demanding an equal share of wealth and power in this world.

The Industrial Revolution and the development of the political economic order known as *capitalism* marked a critical historical shift for Marx in the dialectical march of history. His analysis of this shift began with a radical answer to the philosophical and economic question of what gives an object its value. Earlier theories had argued that value was an inherent quality of objects, or that it was determined by the relative scarcity or abundance of the substances from which an object was made. But Marx saw the flaws in these arguments, and argued instead that the value of an object was not tied to its material substance but rather to the amount of labor it took to produce it. The value of labor, in turn, was equivalent to the value of the resources required to keep a laborer alive and laboring; the value of those resources was tied to the amount of labor it took to produce them, and so on. Labor, in other words, produced value.

Labor, for Marx, was also the defining activity of humanity. It was what set people apart from other creatures, whose activity, unlike that of humans, lacked the conscious use of tools to problem solve and reflexively respond to changing circumstances. In preindustrial economies, most goods were made by individuals working with their hands in small shops. Workers ideally owned (but also typically were rented or lent) their tools, and retained (some) control over the goods they produced, except in the case of slavery or extreme forms of indentured servitude, which Marx also denounced. The difference between what it cost a worker to produce an item (its *use value*) and what it could be sold for (its *exchange value*) was its *surplus value* (or profit). In cases where surplus value was a reward of labor, the system could be characterized as a relatively just one that gave labor dignity and meaning.

But the economic logic of the early Industrial Revolution obliterated this possibility. The development of machines that could manufacture goods at a rate of efficiency and at a cost that was far less than what an individual worker or a guild of workers could make with their own hands meant that workers no longer controlled the means of production. They could no longer make goods at a price that other people would pay, and so lost their means of support. Deprived of the new tools of production—steam-driven machines—they were forced to sell not goods that they produced, but their own labor in order to survive. And the price of their labor in a time before collective bargaining was not related to the market price of the goods produced, but literally was based on no more than what it took to keep workers alive to operate factory owners' machines another day. Moreover, the activities of the factory laborer were no longer meaningful or creative. People no longer made things; now machines did. All that the laborer did was autonomically feed the machines the materials that they needed to produce. Factory laborers were thus doubly *alienated*, not only from the surplus value of their labor that factory owners now kept, but from directive control over their labor and the meaning that the use of those tools had formerly brought to their lives.

Marx's reading of Hegel led him to argue that an economic system that denied the humanity of workers would produce its own revolution in time. He believed this would come in the form of a mass uprising in which workers would appropriate the tools, or means of production of modern industry and, through conscious reflection, devise a new economic order in which workers communally owned and directed the factories they worked in and once again enjoyed the dignity of the surplus value of their own labor.

Since the collapse of the Soviet Union and the rise of market-driven economies in nominally communist states like China and Viet Nam, the world has popularly come to see Marxism as an anachronistic and outdated political and economic philosophy. Yet three concepts developed by Marx remain vital to an understanding of social theory today. The first is historical materialism, particularly the idea that human history is produced through the reflexive response of human beings to situations largely of human origin, and not through any spiritual motivating force—an idea that has led social theorists to describe the origin and dynamics of social relations and development, including language, in material, concrete terms. A second, related concept is the idea that viable political and economic systems are structured to "reproduce the means of production"—that is, institutions within a society are structured to ensure the stability of their social class order over generations, so that the wealthy are socialized to remain wealthy and the poor and working class are socialized by society to remain poor and working class. This is a critical theme, for example, in explaining differences in school achievement and outcomes across social classes. The third continuing contribution of Marxism to social theory is the labor theory of value and its discussion of labor as a tool-using activity that brings dignity and meaning to human life.

### Charles Darwin

In the same decades of the mid-nineteenth century that Marx wrote his principal works, the naturalist Charles Darwin published his theory of evolution in *The Origin of Species* (1939; first published 1859). The principles of Darwinian evolution are widely understood and will not be discussed in detail here. However, Darwin's theory has made and continues to make two vital contributions to social theoretical arguments. The first is the biological, scientific support that it provides for materialist theories of human behavior and social development. Before Darwin, human beings were considered to be a species apart from the natural world, and a species whose most vital qualities, such as language, consciousness, and personality, were of divine rather than biological, natural origin. Darwin's theory opened the possibility of entire new fields of science, such as psychology and linguistics, in which these attributes might be examined and explained in natural, material terms.

Darwin's second contribution to contemporary social theory has been the metaphor of evolution as a reflexive process in which organisms are shaped by, and in turn shape, their surrounding environment. Darwin's description of the reciprocity of causal relations that permeate the ecology of the physical environment was extended by later philosophers such as John Dewey to the description of relations between individuals and their social and cultural environment, and was also highly influential in the formulation of Marxist-based schools of psychology within the Soviet Union in the 1930s.

### Ferdinand de Saussure

Unlike Marx and Darwin, Ferdinand de Saussure was a relatively unknown Swiss scholar who published little in his lifetime, and whose teaching and posthumously published notes on language and meaning, which he termed *semiology*, contained neither the revolutionary social awareness of Marx nor the potential for cultural upheaval and public controversy of Darwin. Saussure's contributions to contemporary social theory derive from his posthumously published lecture notes for his General Course on Language (1966; first published 1916) at the University of Geneva, and can be explained through the elaboration of three principles. The first of these is the distinction that Saussure made in his lectures between *la parole*, or spoken language, and what he termed *la langue*, or language as an abstract system for constructing meaning. Saussure realized that speech, or the actual use of language in real situations, was strongly influenced by a broad range of situational variables to the extent that in speaking situations, meaning was as much influenced by tone, inflection, paralinguistic gestures, timing, and social context as it was by lexical and grammatical choice. This realization led him to reject the possibility of studying actual speech in any systematic, scientific manner, and instead to focus on analyzing language as a pure, logical system.

In Saussure's linguistics, language functions through the manipulation of two sets of relations. One of these is the *paradigmatic* component, which consists of a lexicon of *signs,* or meaning-bearing entities. In common parlance, we would typically refer to these as "words," although in some languages they might be better construed as morphemes, or simply units of meaning. The other is the *syntagmatic* component, which consists of a set of rules for producing complex meanings by placing signs in orderly relation to one another—a "grammar," in common parlance, which produces strings of signs that in Indo-European linguistic contexts are called "sentences."

The second principle to understanding Saussure's linguistics and its contribution to social theory is his description of the *sign*. For Saussure, signs are *dyadic*—that is, they consist of an association between two parts, a "sound image," or *signifier*, constructed of one or more phonemes, or spoken sounds (the sound of "cat" as the blending of three individual sounds, for example), attached by social convention to a general concept or idea (a feline animal, or instance, or in jazz-age slang, someone in close touch with its cultural style), or a *signified*, a concept of an object in the world, be it something concrete like your pet or favorite musician, or in the case of other signs, a more abstract manifestation, such as love or anger. Saussure termed these concrete objects a sign's *referent*.

The third principle of Saussure's linguistics is that the relation between a signifier (a sound image) and a signified (a concept) in a sign is *arbitrary*—that is, there is no logical or causal connection between the two. Instead, the signifier and signified are connected by historical use and by social convention. Thus, even though the sound image /dog/ in English and the sound image /chien/ in French are very different, they are both largely bound to the same concept of an animal and, in bilingual contexts, may even have the same referent. Saussure's description of the sign thus accounts for the infinite variety of both signifieds and signifiers across multiple languages, as well as for differences between languages in referents (the dozens of different words in Inuit for a single English word like "snow," for example, or differences in the names of colors across languages and cultures) and the difficulties this produces for accurate translation.

Saussure's contributions to social theory do not come directly from these principles, however, but rather from the ideas they provoked in the work of later scholars. Playing on the idea of language as a system for producing meaning through the structural interplay among elements, a broad range of sociologists, anthropologists, and literary and popular culture theorists later extended these principles to analyze other structures of human culture, such as kinship systems, buildings, religious rites, novels, and gender relations. Saussure's claim that speech was beyond systematic analysis challenged other linguists to look for patterns and for methods of analysis that would produce systematic descriptions, if not explanations with predictive power, of the use of language within full social contexts. Saussure's work has thus had a profound impact on multiple schools of social theory, from structuralism to poststructuralism and postmodernism, and in the areas of sociolinguistics and discourse analysis. In sum, Saussure's work has influenced contemporary social theory more directly and to nearly as great an extent as Marx and Darwin.

### Friedrich Nietzsche

Perhaps no philosopher of the nineteenth century has been more misused and misunderstood in the twentieth century than Friedrich Nietzsche (1955, 2006). A minor figure in his own lifetime whose work did not sell well, Nietzsche stands in stark contrast to the rational, somber, scholarly vision projected by Marx, Darwin, and Saussure. While the previous three figures were largely the product of Enlightenment rationality and strove to reason carefully and make full use of evidence in support of their arguments, Nietzsche tended to write aphoristically, making pronouncements and leaving an impression on readers through the use of catch words and phrases like his description of the *Übermensch* (translated crudely as the "super man") or "the will to power," a phrase that was picked up by the Nazis after his death and twisted to their own purposes. He stood almost against reason, choosing to dance around the ponderous responsibilities of rationality, and instead using literary and stylistic approaches that were poetic in their effect, and searching for insights and relations that were beyond reason, but that after the fact could be found (or *made*—hence, his unfortunate attraction to the Nazis) to be reasonable.

Nietzsche's contribution to contemporary social theory is not so much through the substance of his work, therefore, but through its style, which strives to produce leaps of insight that escape convention. What Nietzsche provided later philosophers was the means and the will to be playful about their analyses of other scholars' texts, and to be on occasion outrageous in their pronouncements, to provoke people to see the world in a new way, and then to look for ways that the world itself might be changed. He had a direct influence on the work of Michel Foucault and Jacques Derrida, and his spirit can also be discerned in the ritual theory of Victor Turner and in the work of popular culture theorists such as John Fiske.

### Other influential figures

Beyond these four figures, multiple other humanists and social scientists contributed to discourses of the nineteenth century that are remembered or that remain strongly influential today. One figure, for example, who is remembered and whose ideas continue to influence not social theory but the discourses of social policy is Herbert Spencer (1894), who drew from the work of another social theorist, Thomas Malthus, and later from Darwin, to argue that social class hierarchy was determined by the genetic superiority of the upper classes over the lower. Although Spencer never used the term that is closely associated with his name, *Social Darwinism*, he did coin the phrase *the survival of the fittest* in his justification of not only the class system but governmental neglect of the poor and working class. Even though his ideas are publicly repudiated today, they continue to have an insidious, hidden effect at times on educational policy.

Two more positive early influences on the development of social theory today are the German political historian Max Weber (1962) and the French sociologist and educator Emile Durkheim (Thompson 1985). Along with Marx, both Weber and Durkheim focused on the analysis of contemporary social phenomena in macrostructural terms, and are considered the founders of modern sociology. Their analytical approaches and epistemological grounding—their theories of how we know and how knowledge is produced—were quite distinctive, however. After the French philosopher and sociologist Auguste Comte, Durkheim was a *positivist*, who believed that social science research grounded in practices similar to those of the physical sciences could reveal objective knowledge that could then rationally be used to improve society. Weber, on the other hand, was an *antipositivist*, who argued that human social behavior was inherently different in its dynamics than the behavior of physical objects, and that its study required more humanistically oriented approaches, such as comparative analysis of historical periods and cultures. Using very different approaches, both men produced seminal studies of social phenomena, Durkheim on suicide, for example, and Weber on bureaucracy and religion, that are influential to this day and that continue to shape social theory and social science research. Together, their perspectives form two methodological poles around which social science research is performed today.

## Discourses of social theory

Contemporary social theory is the product of a tangle of ideas forwarded in the nineteenth century by a wide range of both humanistically and scientifically oriented scholars, which were formulated both in critique of, and in response to, the rational idealism of the eighteenth century and its technological and social consequences. As a result, it is itself a field of disparate theories of multiple origins, with little unity and, as I noted in the introduction to this chapter, a rhetorical style that is often daunting to the uninitiated reader.

However, as its ideas are used to inform educational research, social theory is also not without central themes around which an organized and relatively coherent discussion of major ideas and perspectives can be organized. With the strong caveat to readers that the following discussion of these ideas forms only the barest introduction to the principal works of social theory, and the invitation to readers to move beyond this chapter to reading the primary texts of the theorists I discuss here and their major commentators, I present a discussion of the principal theoretical perspectives of social theory organized around four pivots: language, discourse, meaning, and practice.

### Language

The question of what language is and how it is acquired by young children has been a topic of intense theorization and controversy from the early twentieth century to the present. In earlier conceptions of human "nature," language, like thought itself, was typically regarded as a divine gift to humans, a metaphysical property beyond physical causality or explanation. Systematic, focused research and theorization about language began with the emergence of psychology as a field of study in the late nineteenth and early twentieth centuries. Behaviorists such as B. F. Skinner in the USA argued that language was acquired as a conditioned response to environmental stimuli. The reinforcement, or reward, that children were given by parents and others when they imitated words and phrases fixed the association of words with objects in their memories. Developmentalists and nativists such as Piaget in Europe and Chomsky in the USA, on the other hand, argued that the capacity for language was an innate biological and genetic characteristic of humans. They argued that infants' natural babbling and "egocentric speech" gave way, through processes of socialization, to the development of true speech and the development of thoughts, as children strove to solve problems within their environment.

A more radical theory of language acquisition was proposed by the Soviet developmental psychologist Lev Vygotsky and his team in the 1930s, but not widely known in the West until its publication in English translation in *Thought and Language* (1986, first published 1962). Vygotsky's theory was grounded in Marxist principles of historical materialism and in Darwinian principles of evolution, that is, in a view of human development produced through the human species' dialectical struggle over time with the physical and social environment. In this materialist view of language, words function as acoustical objects, while syntax is acquired as a *practice*, or culturally and historically motivated pattern of activity. These are "picked up" by young children who exercise their evolutionary, genetic predisposition for using tools to use words in the same manner that one might use a stone or a stick: As a device for *mediating* an interaction between oneself and the world in order to obtain a goal.

At first, according to Vygotsky, speech and thought are external, that is, children talk out loud and their talking parallels their thought processes. The externalization of thought and speech makes it easier for young children to manipulate words as tools, and remains a feature of human behavior into adulthood. Think, for example, about the last time you had difficulty opening a package or assembling a child's toy or you struggled to read something that didn't make sense to you. Did you catch yourself mumbling as you struggled to fit parts together or to connect one word to the next? This phenomenon in children, called *subvocalization*, was taken by Vygotsky as an indication that the child was struggling to make sense of a situation "mentally," or through internal thought processes, and so thought and the use of language had re-emerged temporarily, to make them easier to manipulate as tools.

For Vygotsky, thinking and speaking in early childhood were parallel externalized processes that, over time and practice, became largely internalized, or cognitive, and convergent. In the process of internalization, the tools of language became *signs*—not "real objects" of the external world anymore, but internal, semiotic images that bore the traces of their history of use, not only by individuals, but by all those individuals from whom the child had first picked them up, by the individuals from whom those individuals had gotten them, and so on, down through the history of language and language use.

A second Soviet-era theorist of language is the philosopher and literary scholar, Mikhail Bakhtin (1981; see also Holquist 2002). Like Vygotsky, Bakhtin's theoretical perspective on language, its origins, and its use as a tool of human meaning-making is grounded in historical materialism. But whereas Vygotsky was considered relatively orthodox in his appropriation of Marxist principles and their application to developmental psychology (perhaps because Vygotsky died young, in 1934, of tuberculosis), Bakhtin's uses of Marxism wandered farther afield, and away from Stalinist ideology. As a result, he and his work frequently suffered from state repression, to the point that during his life Bakhtin was denied his doctorate, sentenced to a labor camp in Siberia (he appealed on the grounds of bad health and was sent to Kazakhstan instead), and sometimes had to disguise the authorship of his work in order to have it published.

Like Vygotsky, Bakhtin held that language was the material of thought. It was a tool whose use in the present bore the traces of its use historically, along with past meanings and connotations. History and culture lived in and through language for Bakhtin, so much so that his writings at times seem to have an almost mystical, if not spiritual, tone about them (in fact, he was exiled to Kazakhstan for his association with the Russian Orthodox Church). As a literary scholar, Bakhtin's unit of analysis was not words but *utterances*—propositional statements that bore the traces of history in their construction and meaning—and his central concern was not with cognitive processes but instead with the processes of history, politics, and literature.

Bakhtin departed from the orthodoxy of the Soviet era in his use of the term *dialogism* rather than *dialectic* to describe language processes in-use and across historical time and space. As Bakhtin used it, the term connotes many of the same meanings as the English word *dialogue*, but extends far beyond the sense of a conversation between two individuals to describe patterns of exchange in language and concepts at societal, cultural, and ultimately historical levels as well, both through speech and through the literary form at the center of much of Bakhtin's work, the novel. Dialogism is the central concept in Bakhtin's theorizing about the role of language in providing both social and cultural stability and change across time and space. Within a dialogic world, the collective voices of humanity circulate in speech and in writing, appropriating each other's utterances and using them sometimes as they were initially intended, and sometimes differently.

In this idealized world, which Bakhtin argued, is made present in the novels of Dostoyevsky and others, language is *polyphonic*, meaning that the social world is composed of multiple voices whose utterances speak from many different points of view. The continuity of language and of ideas across time and space is maintained by *centripetal* forces, such as the transmission across time of the material of language—the sounds of words and utterances; the graphics of written language—in oral stories and poems and written texts, for example, that tend to solidify the meaning of signs. Bakhtin's concept of the *chronotope*, a "time–space" configuration such as a narrative motif within a novel or the binding of particular time and space within a culture's narratives (think, for example, of "9/11" as the shorthand term for all that happened around the collapse of the Twin Towers) is also a critical centripetal linguistic force, one that lends stability to meanings over time. Change in language and ideas over time and space is promoted through *centrifugal* forces, such as changing material and social circumstances, uses of language by variant novelists and other writers and speakers, and by the condition of *heteroglossia*, or the coexistence of many varieties of language use—multiple dialects, multiple meanings of words, multiple words with overlapping meanings, multiple registers—within a single language.

Against this dialogic image of liberatory, open exchange among speakers across time and space, Bakhtin poses the image of a monologic world, in which through force or intimidation, one voice, one point of view, one authoritarian monologue, prevails. Although Bakhtin did not use this image in direct critique of patterns of language use within the Stalinist state, the comparison was obvious enough in his time for Soviet authorities to view his work in dissident terms, and to respond accordingly, by exile and later by appointing Bakhtin, who was surely one of the greatest scholars of Russian literature in the twentieth century, to a position in an obscure university for most of his career.

The moral and ethical implications of Bakhtin's work on patterns of language use and communication have made it attractive to researchers interested in theorizing how patterns of classroom interaction among students and between teacher and students might be made freer and more open— that is, in Bakhtinian terms, more *polyphonic* (Lensmire 2000). Traditional classroom instruction has been regarded as largely authoritarian and monologic. Teachers are seen to possess knowledge, which they transmit through lectures and the controlled distribution of texts, and students are viewed as the receivers of this knowledge, whose accurate transmission is measured through tests and other forms of assessment. Even when students are permitted to speak, the typical pattern is one controlled entirely by the teacher, who calls on students and evaluates their responses (Cazden 2001). Bakhtin's work provides a counter scenario, one in which the productive use of language is dialogic, and depends on a patterning of all voices in unfettered exchange of language and ideas.

## Discourse

The term *discourse* is a critical feature of a wide range of social theorists' work, but also one with nearly as many specific definitions as it has theorists. Generally, however, when social theorists use the term they are typically referring to a series of extended exchanges among multiple speakers or writers, either within relatively contained contexts, such as classrooms, homes, or instances of public interaction, or to a broader series of exchanges in more distanced contexts, such as the mass media, public policy debates, or academic fields such as education, history, or chemistry. Moreover, their analyses may involve not only the words, or the text, of these exchanges, but also an analysis of stylistic aspects of the discourse, such as speakers' tone and gestures, the timing of exchanges, and other written and oral rhetorical devices. As in Bakhtin's work, a central theme in the theorization of discourse is the ways that people's uses of language in both local social contexts and broader, societal contexts determine what is considered true and valuable, and by extension, who has the power to make these determinations.

Within Anglo-American contexts, James Gee (2005, 2007) is the best-known and most frequently cited theorist of discourse at the local, interpersonal level. In much of his work Gee has focused on explaining differences in academic achievement among working class and linguistic minority students and students from middle-class homes who spoke the dialect of English typical of the professional managerial culture. Gee argued that habits of speech, including not only accent and word choice but also knowledge of the rules of exchange—when to speak, how to phrase comments, what to speak about, how to stand, how loudly or softly to speak, and so on—were acquired early in childhood within one's home community, and were an essential part of individuals' identities, not only for themselves but for others.

Use of professional managerial discourse—the discourse of power and authority in modern society—signaled membership within that group with all its privileges and trajectory for academic and professional success, while the use of other dialects signaled otherness to the group in power, who regarded the uses of other discourses as signs of linguistic, cognitive, and social inferiority. In this way, language was used to differentiate among social and ethnic groups, and so reproduce social inequality within society. Moreover, for Gee, the patterns of discourse that one acquired early in life were nearly indelible. Growing up, a child from a working class or linguistic minority background might work to try to acquire the discursive mannerisms of the professional managerial class, but her or his success would always be only partial. Even if a child from such a background were to function within the professional managerial class as an adult, she or he would always feel somewhat estranged from it, and would always be identifiable by subtle signs of her or his former discursive group.

Gee has also frequently been cited for the distinction he makes between discourse as language in-use, which he labels "little d" discourse, and discourse as a broader societal and academic phenomenon, which he labels "big D" Discourse. A second theory of discourse, and one that expands Gee's concept of Discourse into its broadest meaning, is found in the work of the French philosopher of history and sociology, Michel Foucault (1980). Foucault's views may have been shaped in part by his encounters with the medical profession, both through his father, who was a surgeon and wanted Foucault to join his practice, and through his experiences as a psychiatric patient in his twenties when he suffered from bouts of depression as a student at the Ecole Normale Supérieure in Paris. A central theme of Foucault's historical research was the history of social deviance and its treatment across historical periods, or *epochs* (1977). Foucault argued that the distinction between who was "normal" and who was "deviant" in society, and how the deviant should be treated shifted abruptly from one period of history to the next, in accordance with the logic, or systems of thought, that prevailed within an historical period. This logic was disseminated throughout society not only in written texts and public discussions but through its physical enactment in the architectural design of prisons and schools and in the development of institutional practices—military drills, medical and academic examinations, schedules—meant to discipline and control the masses both physically and mentally by rewarding consistency, or "normality," and punishing or otherwise remediating deviance. Thus, through discourses of medicine, education, criminology, and the like, people's identities were constituted, and they were treated, and learned to behave, accordingly. Discourse for Foucault became an almost supralinguistic force, one that permeated every aspect of people's lives, was virtually inescapable, and through which the power to control and channel the thoughts, desires, and actions of individuals was disseminated.

A third discourse theorist, Norman Fairclough (1995, 2003), has developed a theory and method of critical discourse analysis (CDA) that draws from not only Foucault and Bakhtin, but from multiple other social theorists, including Saussure and Habermas (see below), and that focuses on the analysis of "texts"—in Fairclough's definition, sections of writing or speech—within the social and cultural contexts in which they are produced, circulated, and read, or consumed. Fairclough's goal, in a sense, is to combine strategies for analyzing the discourses of everyday language use (Gee's discourse) within the larger Discursive contexts (in Foucault's use of the word) in which they appear. His method of analysis is used to demonstrate the ways in which mundane forms of communication, such as newspaper articles, selections from school textbooks, and teachers' interactions with students, do the social and cultural, or *ideological*, work of shaping and maintaining normative or state-sanctioned views of reality about what is true or false, right or wrong, or worthy or unworthy of attention (e.g. views about the logic and objectivity of achievement testing, or the logic of streaming students according to "ability"). It is "critical" because the goal of these analyses is to expose and demonstrate the ill-logic of the ideological perspective of official Discourses as they are practiced in local discourse settings.

An equally critical but theoretically and methodologically very different approach to discourse and its analysis has been proposed by the German philosopher Jürgen Habermas (1984). Habermas is a postwar member of the Frankfurt School of social philosophy, a group of philosophers who stridently opposed the Nazi regime in Germany. In their analysis, they described the rationalism and systematicity of the Nazis as the result of a separation between *subjectivity* (our understanding of reality as a result of personal experience) and *objectivity* (what exists and is "real" outside of human perception or experience) and the subsequent privileging of rational objectivity within Western civilization, a process that began in the eighteenth century during the Enlightenment. The consequence of this separation and privileging of the rational side of human existence, in their view, was not the control of the subjective, emotionally biased side of human life, but instead its sublimation and re-emergence in the rationalization of racism and anti-Semitism, and in "rational solutions" to these problems, such as the death camps of Auschwitz and Dachau.

Although the horrors of Nazism and other twentieth-century ills have been blamed on the internal contradictions of the Enlightenment and modernity by many philosophers, including Foucault and several others yet to be discussed in this chapter, Habermas has taken a different approach to this issue. Like these social theorists, he, too, is horrified by the "solutions" that an over-rationalized, *instrumentalist* approach have brought to the world, but unlike them, he has not rejected modernism itself. Instead, Habermas describes modernity as an "incomplete" project that needs to be clarified and revised rather than rejected. For Habermas, this revision begins with two sets of distinctions. The first is between *rationality* (a hyper-objective approach that denies the possibility that logic itself might be biased by culture or history) and *reason* (a more pragmatic, socially balanced approach that relies on the use of evidence and public argument). The second set is among three different *ontological realms*, or forms of existence, in the world: the *objective/physical realm*, which deals with facts about the physical world that can be cross-validated through multiple points of access (e.g. the study of chemical, biological, or geophysical phenomena); the *normative-evaluative realm,* which pertains to legal and social arrangements arrived at through consensus about what should or ought to be; and the *subjective realm,* which pertains to artistic expressions and personal beliefs that can only be scrutinized using internal, personal criteria.

Each of these three realms, according to Habermas, produces arguments about the nature of the aspect of reality they address (physical reality; social reality; personal reality) which are in their own way either valid or invalid, *depending on criteria that are specific to each realm.* In other words, the validity, or truthfulness, of a statement made about some physical phenomenon (e.g. a cause of cancer) is determinable using criteria and a method that is different from the criteria used to judge the validity of a normative statement (e.g. a law banning smoking in public spaces), or the criteria used to judge a personal, subjective perspective (e.g. one's response to cigarette smoke). Habermas argues that problems typically arise within modernity when the logic and criteria of the objective/physical realm are mistakenly used to validate policy decisions, without benefit of open public discussion about their normative/evaluative rightness or validity, particularly when what are described as "facts" are actually heavily biased by subjective viewpoints.

Habermas argues further that the remedy to these problems is the establishment within modern societies of opportunities for open, public discourse about societal problems—spaces for what he terms *communicative action,* in which parties with multiple points of view come together, and through an honest exchange of evidence and arguments, strive *intersubjectively* to understand each others' points of view and so arrive at consensual agreement about a course of social action, such as a change of social policy. Habermas draws from the speech act theory of two Anglo–American philosophers of language-in-use, J. L. Austin (1975) and John Searle (1969) in support of his argument. Austin and Searle argued that language is not merely something that human beings do to "express themselves"; it is, more importantly, a tool for taking action on the world by placing oneself and one's actions in relation to others within the world. For example, if I say to you, "I wish you'd skip to Chapter Three," I'm not just expressing an empty thought; I am *willing* that you do something—pressing you to act in a certain way. Similarly, a simple greeting, "Good morning, how are you?" is not a simple expression; it's an act that draws attention, that brings the listener into personal contact with the speaker. Even a statement such as "It's raining outside," when directed toward someone, is an action that brings a particular fact into conversational play, and presumably for a reason.

Speech acts have force, or do work in the world, because of the pragmatic, socially acquired predisposition that speakers have to strive toward understanding, a predisposition and ability that Habermas terms *communicative competence*. We want to make sense of what others have said and to be understood ourselves; and so, through countless exchanges in a lifetime, we develop a normative presumption that what is said to us and what we say to others should be purposeful and forthright. However, through (hopefully, fewer, but more memorable) negative experiences, we also begin to develop tacit criteria and practices for determining when a speaker's reasoning is flawed or deceptive, and so not communicative, in Habermas's terms, but *strategic*—that is, not aimed at finding intersubjective understanding, but at achieving a self-interested goal.

Habermas's Theory of Communicative Action can be summed up in a quote from Abraham Lincoln: "You may fool all the people some of the time, you can even fool some of the people all of the time, but you cannot fool all of the people all the time." By requiring speakers within a public forum to reveal their reasoning processes and full evidence, and by applying criteria that are relevant to the ontological realm (objective/physical, normative-evaluative, or subjective) about which an argument is being made, the validity of statements can be examined and determined to be true or not true, right or wrong, appropriate or inappropriate. For this reason, it is a powerful analytical tool for examining, for example, the logic of policy statements about educational programs and practices—that is, for testing whether decisions made about curriculum content and instructional practices are warranted by the reasons and evidence provided by policy makers in their support.

Finally, Thomas Kuhn, a philosopher of science, analyzed shifts in scientific knowledge as discursive in their processes. In his classic study, *The Structure of Scientific Revolutions* (1996, first published 1962), Kuhn argued that in the natural sciences theories precede rather than follow empirical investigations and that the function of empirical investigation has been less to generate fresh theoretical insight than to validate or extend what has already been assumed to be accurate, or true. Moreover, for Kuhn the development of theoretical understanding within the physical sciences has not followed a pattern of gradual and steady accumulation of experimentally produced "facts" that dialectically alters the contours of theory over time. Rather, it has followed a pattern in which experiments and other empirical investigations are designed to preserve and elaborate upon theoretical assumptions—that is, almost as hedges *against* the threats to intellectual claims and professional careers that more dissonant findings might produce—until the weight of countermanding evidence becomes so great that a rupture, or revolution, in understanding occurs—a revolution that is given order and stability not through revision of the old theory, but by the reconstitution of knowledge through a new set of intuitions that seem finally to offer an explanation beyond reasonable doubt.

## Meaning

A set of questions explored by social theorists that is even more basic than the question of how spoken and written language works focuses on how human beings coordinate and make sense of the multiple forms of sensory input in their environment—through sight, touch, sound, taste, and smell—that are extralinguistic; in other words, questions about how we make/give meaning from, and to, the world. To grasp the significance of these questions, imagine that you are abducted by aliens from another dimension and are whisked off to their world, where you discover that the most basic points of reference—what is up and down; how things feel, smell, look, taste, sound—are all so radically different that you can't get your bearings or distinguish where one thing leaves off and another begins. How would you begin to make sense of this strange new environment? How would you understand or communicate with, or even recognize, your captors? How would you begin to develop some familiarity with this environment, so that you might be able to predict and gain at least a sense of control over what was going to happen next?

The question of how we give meaning to the world, both linguistically and extralinguistically, is a central question for many different schools of social theory. In this section I will briefly outline three very different perspectives—of Wittgenstein, the hermeneutics of Hans-Georg Gadamer, and structuralism—plus a fourth, poststructuralism, which extends and elaborates on the third, and two of its most common variants: postcolonialism and poststructural feminism/queer theory.

The first of these approaches is that taken by the Austrian philosopher and Cambridge professor, Ludwig Wittgenstein (1922, 1953). Wittgenstein's early education was in engineering, where he demonstrated a considerable talent for mathematics, and later, the philosophy of mathematics. Like his Cambridge mentor Bertrand Russell, Wittgenstein took the position in his early work that logic was mathematical in its processes, and that the solution of seemingly intractable philosophical problems could only come through analytical methods as precise as those of mathematics—methods that were stymied not by logic but rather by the imprecision of human language. Throughout history, philosophers had tried to solve problems through the use of propositional statements meant to represent abstract conditions. But the propositions themselves, when removed from the context of their use and logically examined, proved to be illogical, or "nonsense," as Wittgenstein puts it. Philosophy, therefore, should not be about solving problems but about clarifying their logic; and it should avoid explication of big problems (which requires language and many leaps of faith about causal and associative relationships) in favor of active demonstration, practices that Wittgenstein apparently believed he was engaging in through the use of symbolic logic within the text of the only book he published in his lifetime, the *Tractatus Logico-Philosophicus* (1922; Monk 1990).

In the second half of his career, however, Wittgenstein's explorations led in a very different direction. In *Philosophical Investigations* (1953), which was posthumously edited and published by his students, Wittgenstein again showed the meaninglessness of words in and of themselves. And yet, he also noted, although words do not mean in themselves, they do *convey* meaning, and do so very well *within the contexts of their use*. How can this be?

It is not through grammar and semantics alone, for these, too, are abstractions with no meaning outside the context of their use. For example, suppose as you're reading this the telephone rings. You answer, and a voice says, "It's five o'clock." What does that mean? You look at your watch: No, it's only 2:30. "What do you mean, 'It's five o'clock?'" you ask. "It's five o'clock," the voice says. You begin to wonder: Perhaps you're late for something. Perhaps the person has the wrong number. At any rate, you have no way of knowing what is meant; the sentence should mean something *beyond* what you've decoded, but without a context, you're lost. Now, however suppose you're fast asleep in a hotel somewhere and the telephone rings. You answer it and a voice says, "It's five o'clock." You know immediately what that means: It's time to get up.

According to Wittgenstein, language is a *game* that people learn to play, typically not through formal instruction, but through daily involvement in the contexts of its use (Rundle 1990). As a game, it is governed by normative rules, some of which involve the ordering of the game itself, and some of which order the contexts in which the game is to be played but whose players consensually recognize and abide by, more or less. The rules that govern contexts of use and so the conveyance of meaning are seldom formal or written down; they operate more as heuristics, or rules of thumb. Moreover, according to Brenner (1999), these rules and games are pragmatic in their development, their enforcement, and their interpretation over changing circumstances; they are less like the rules that professional athletes play by than the rules that govern pick-up games of basketball or sandlot baseball.

In his own lifetime, the logical rigor with which Wittgenstein pursued his investigations did much to dispel the lingering notion that language was or could be made a transparent medium for constructing meaning, particularly within mathematics and the sciences. Although today Wittgenstein's work has only an indirect impact on social theory, his pragmatic focus on examining linguistic phenomena within the contexts of their use was taken up by later scholars, including Jürgen Habermas, and speech act theorists, as well as by Wittgenstein's student Stephen Toulmin (1958, 1990, 2001), whose analysis of argumentation in everyday contexts will be discussed further in Chapter Two.

An equally pragmatic but philosophically unrelated approach to the production of meaning is the *hermeneutics* of Hans-Georg Gadamer, a German philosopher of the early to mid-twentieth century. Very briefly, the term *hermeneutics* refers to a process of interpretation, in which a reader interprets, or determines the meaning, of a statement through a process of comparison with the statements that surround it within a given context. The term originally referred to practices of biblical scholarship, but has since been expanded to the analysis of other forms of text, including written and visual texts, and to the interpretation of sociological and cultural events.

Gadamer described the process of interpretation as the fusion of the interpreter's *horizon*—the totality of her or his experiences and knowledge at the moment of interpretation—with the horizon of the text—the totality of knowledge about the text and its history. In this process, interpretation develops as the individual parts of a text (its sentences, or images, or within a social event, its moments) are recognized as a whole and then as each is related back to the whole. This constant circular process of relating part to whole and whole to part was termed the *hermeneutic circle,* by Gadamer. Hermeneutic approaches to understanding social events have had a strong impact on ethnographic approaches to educational research and evaluation, and are particularly prominent in the work of methodologists such Carspecken (1996) and Schwandt (2002).

The school, or approach to understanding meaning-making processes with the farthest-ranging impact with social science research, however, is one grounded in the *structuralist* linguistic principles of Ferdinand de Saussure. Beginning in the 1920s, linguists in Russia and later, in the 1930s and 1940s, in Prague, applied the basic principles of Saussure's work to the analysis of narrative genres, such as folk tales (Propp 1968). Saussure's analysis of language as a paradigmatic system of elements (a "vocabulary") arranged syntagmatically (by a "grammar") into complex and coherent ideational units ("sentences") was broadened by these theorists to describe narrative elements (characters; settings; events) arranged in a temporal, narrative sequence. The French anthropologist Claude Lévi-Strauss, who was influenced by members of the Prague School as a refugee living in New York during World War II, introduced structuralism into ethnographic analysis in the 1950s with the publication of *Tristes Tropiques* and *Structural Anthropology* (English translations in 1967 and 1963, respectively).

A critical part of Lévi-Strauss's theory and analytical method, which he took from the Prague School's analysis of the phonology, or sound-system, of languages, was the idea that the elements of a system of meaning are distinguished from each other through a system of oppositional binary pairs. Phonemes, or individual sounds of language, can be distinguished as voiced (made through the use of the vocal cords) or unvoiced; aspirated (producing a puff of breath) or unaspirated (little or no puff), and so on. Lévi-Strauss noted that the same binary logic prevails in the ways that cultures he studied in Brazil and elsewhere made sense of the world around them, that is, as a set of binary oppositions such as sun/moon, night/day, male/female, north/south, east/west and so on. Moreover, in the stories of these cultures the binary pairs "lined up" in association with each other, such as in the common association of male:sun:day v. the common association of female:moon:night. His analysis led him to conclude that he had discovered a fundamental, universal principle of human cognition, and one that was cosmological in its capacity to connect human sense-making with organizational structures, not only across human cultures but within the natural environment.

The central idea of structuralism, that there is a cognitively structured "architecture" of human sense-making and cultural production analogous to the architecture of language (a set of elements organized by a set of grammatical rules, or principles), was soon taken up by many different disciplines in the humanities, fine arts, and social sciences, and applied to the structural analysis of archaeological sites, houses, cities, paintings and all sorts of visual art, social class, and many different public and semi-public spaces, such as gardens, churches, classrooms, and, in my own research, school libraries (Dressman 1997). Throughout the 1960s and early 1970s, structuralism was a dominant force in the work of several major French social theorists, including Michel Foucault and Pierre Bourdieu (see below), and remains central to the recent and ongoing efforts of Kress and van Leeuwen (2006) to develop a "grammar" of visual imagery in Western culture.

But structuralism's all-inclusiveness, its apparent capacity to explain human culture and cognition in such basic, universal terms, and most important, its implication that human beings are collectively locked into seeing and acting in the world through the logic of binary opposition—a "prison-house of language," in the words of critic Frederic Jameson (1975)—soon brought it into close scrutiny by other scholars. The most penetrating of these was from the French literary critic and philosopher of language, Jacques Derrida, who first introduced his philosophy of language to an Anglophone audience at a conference at Johns Hopkins University.

Derrida (1976) returned to the phonological analysis of structuralism, and argued that in the opposition of the signifier (the sound, or phonic image) /tree/ with /free/, the only way that we can identify /tree/ as one of the pair is to be aware of its contrast with /free/. In other words, although the f-sound is absent in /tree/, its trace must be present in order for the /t/ to be salient to us—it is thus *present in its absence*. This same principle of "absent presence" also pertains for the signified portion of a sign, that is, the concept to which the signifier (the sound, /tree/) is attached. To imagine a tree, in other words, we must also be aware, even in their absence, of the traces of the concepts against which "tree" is contrasted, such as "shrub," or "post," or "grass." Similarly, we cannot conceive of "north" as a concept without "south" being present in its absence, or "male" without "female," and so on.

If every signifier and signified in a language carries with it the trace of its binary opposite(s), then the principle of opposition itself is always threatened, always in danger of *deconstruction,* of collapsing inward under the stress of its own internal contradiction. It therefore takes a great deal of energy and cultural/political work for its linguistic and ideological architecture to be maintained within a culture. Moreover, Derrida also noted, in any binary opposition, the two sides are not equal in social and political power. One side (usually the first of the pair, as in male/female) plays a dominant, "positive" role in relation to its *other*, which it pushes to the margins of cultural discourse and action. Thus, male is *not* female; in English studies, reading is *not* writing; and in educational discourses, theory is *not* practice.

In a series of elegant close readings, or analyses, of literary texts, Derrida demonstrated that conventional, taken-for-granted readings of those texts could be shown to have no more truth-value, or meaning, than readings that reversed or otherwise completely subverted what it was assumed the author "intended" or what readers typically presumed the text to mean. These readings produced shock waves within the academy and within social and political spheres, because, as Derrida argued, deconstruction was not something that one did to a text, but rather something that was "always already" happening within texts themselves. Deconstruction was thus perceived negatively by some conservative academics as bringing the end of meaning, but by the left as a radical up-ending or *decentering* of textual authority and structural rigidity.

The term *poststructuralism* was applied by later scholars to a school of structural analysis based on Derrida's view that binary opposites within the discourses of society are fraught with internal contradiction. Poststructuralism differs from structuralism in its argument that the binaries that structure the social order and our normative sense of reality are not "natural," but rather the product of historic and cultural inequity. Queer theorists and poststructural feminists such as Judith Butler (1990, 1993), for example, have used poststructuralism to show how normative presumptions of the "naturalness" of heterosexuality depend on the discursive maintenance of clear and strict distinctions between male and female bodies and between the *performance* of behaviors characterized as intrinsically "male," and the performance of other behaviors that are characteristically not-male, or female.

Poststructuralist approaches have also been prominent in the establishment of a field of study that focuses on cultural relations between the West and its former colonies in Africa, Asia and the Pacific, and Latin America, known as *postcolonialism*. In *Orientalism* (1978) and later *Culture and Imperialism* (1993), the Palestinian activist and literary scholar Edward Saïd detailed the creation by writers in the nineteenth century of a binary between the West and the East. This was a binary in which the East was portrayed as the exotic, lascivious "other" to a more "civilized" (prudish, sexually disciplined) West—a vessel, in other words, for all the pent-up desire of the Victorian period, and a place in need of conquest and, in the Foucauldian sense, "discipline." Similarly, other postcolonial scholars, such as Mary Louise Pratt in *Imperial Eyes* (1992), examined the travel writings of the first European explorers to make contact with the people of South America and Africa. Pratt argued that in the earliest period, *contact zones* were established in which Europeans and the people of these continents were, for a time, on equal terms—a period that permitted great exchange of goods and ideas (including the very notion of a "Europe" and of democracy, according to Pratt)—but that, again, led to the subsequent establishment of a system of binary oppositions between "civilized" Europe and "savage" new worlds, through the circulation of later travel accounts, and to their eventual conquest.

Another creative and radical set of theories that build on poststructuralist insights are Deleuze and Guattari's (1987) analysis of information and knowledge networks based on the image of the *rhizome* and a related set of theories describing relations among humans and technology, known collectively as *Actor-Network Theory* (or ANT; see Latour 2005). Both Deleuze and Guattari and ANT would dissolve the notion that knowledge and what is meant by "the social" can be adequately represented as relatively stable structures. Instead, both focus not on entities themselves, but on the ways that associations are made among them.

For Deleuze and Guattari, whose work was influenced by Nietzsche as well as poststructuralism, the activity of knowing cannot be represented in vertical, *arborescent* terms, in hierarchical taxonomies, but *rhizomatically*, as a horizontal network of branching associations that spread like the roots of grasses, making connections and moving in multiple directions at once. Within educational research, their work is only recently beginning to have influence, primarily as an approach for challenging conventional modes of data analysis and representation (Rowe and Leander 2006). ANT, which developed from attempts to account for processes of technological and scientific innovation, similarly "reassembles" the definition of "the social" in terms of the networked relations among entities, both human and nonhuman, which are termed *actors* (or sometimes *actants*). In ANT, both human and nonhuman actors have *agency*, or the capacity to act on a situation. This controversial aspect of the theory makes it useful in accounting for the role of computers and other forms of electronic technology within economic, political, and educational fields of activity.

### Practice

The power of poststructuralism lies in the set of strategies it provides to marginalized groups, such as women, religious minorities, the gay, lesbian, and bi/transexual community, people of color, the disabled, or the colonized, to name a few, including adolescents and children (who, as not-adults are also not-responsible and not-rational) and students (who are not-educated), to demonstrate that the binaries naming them as the "other," lesser half of a binary pair are not naturally justified or self-evident, but in fact are part of an artificial, historical process of differentiation whose agenda is to distribute power and resources inequitably within the world. Theoretically, poststructuralism also provides a powerful response to the tendency of structuralist schools of social theory to characterize societies as bleakly *overdetermined*—that is, as systems whose dynamics and processes are constructed in such a totalizing way that a significant shift in power or cultural logic from within is almost impossible to conceive of, much less enact.

For example, Critical Race Theory (CRT; Bell 2004; Ladson-Billings 1995) focuses on the artificiality of racial distinctions and the legal and discursive means by which the White majority in the USA and other former slave-holding nations use race as a category for continuing discriminatory practices, despite—or sometimes as the ironic result of—public liberalist discourses of racial desegregation and integration. In response, a central tenet of CRT is that people of color cannot look to White liberalism as a force working on behalf of their liberation; instead, they must actively work to define and redefine societal and legal relations for themselves.

Structuralist theories grounded in the *semiology* of Ferdinand de Saussure, for example, tend to dismiss the practical, everyday behavior of people in favor of analyzing what are taken to be the underlying principles, or structures of thought and action, that seem to order societies at more abstract—and so, in the logic of modernity, more "real"—levels. Similarly, structuralist theories grounded in Marxists theories of capitalism as an organizing principle of modern society tend toward demonstrating the ways that the multiple institutions of a society—its courts, its schools, its political system—cooperate to *reproduce* the cultural and social differences among capitalists, managers, and workers needed as part of the infrastructure of continuing industrial production.

The work of three major figures in French social theory and research illustrates the application of a combination of both of these structuralist schools to the analysis of cultural institutions. Michel Foucault (1980) argued that within modern society the power to shape and control people's behavior was not exercised through direct force, but through publicly disseminated and accepted discourses that hinged on socially sanctioned distinctions between sanity and insanity, health and sickness, and normative and deviant (criminal) behavior. These discourses, in turn, were part of a set of modern *practices*— of uniformity, examination, even, quite literally, the structural design of institutions—whose purpose was to discipline the bodies, and so the minds, of the mass population. Foucault's most famous example was the *panopticon*—a widely employed architectural design for prisons and asylums, in which a round or octagonal multi-storied building was built with a single ring of transparent cells, or rooms, for one inmate, and a multi-storied tower was constructed in the center of the ring (1977). A doctor or a guard would be stationed on each floor of the tower and, merely by watching (*gazing*, in Foucault's terms), the inmates would be self-consciously pressured into correcting their own habits of behavior. As a metaphor for induced self-inspection, the panopticon can be applied within current educational settings to describe practices such as the classroom intercom (a monitoring device for keeping teachers and students on their toes) and other monitoring devices, from testing programs to charts that record the supposedly "free reading" activities of students in school libraries (Dressman 1997).

Foucault's early mentor in Paris in the 1950s, Louis Althusser (1971), developed a structuralist theory of ideological control that was more direct in its dynamics than Foucault's. Althusser's work built directly on and extended Marx's view of modern social systems as being structurally determined by the needs of industrial production. He described social institutions such as the police, hospitals, the media, and particularly educational systems as *Ideological State Apparatuses*, or ISAs, and held that their primary social function was to habituate individuals to self-identify and so behave in ways consistent with the subjective role they were needed to play within a capitalist society. This process of subjugation, Althusser held, took place through *interpellation*, a discursive process in which individuals were hailed, or called to, as someone within a particular role—as a self-sacrificing teacher, or as a star athlete or "average" student—that, so named and positioned within society, became self-fulfilling in its outcome. Althusser's description of interpellation also bears resemblance to, and may have been influenced by, Italian Marxist Antonio Gramsci's (1988) description of *hegemony*, whereby workers are led by their employers, and by the discourses of the state and religion, to (falsely) reason that capitalism is a just system—or that, even if it isn't, its alternative would have consequences for them and their families even more negative than the circumstances and conditions in which they were already living.

Third, the French anthropologist and sociologist Pierre Bourdieu (1984, 1990; Bourdieu and Passeron 1977) conducted a series of studies of Algerian Berber peasants, the French higher educational system, and relations between social class and aesthetic taste in France, in which he argued that the supposedly free choices people make in arranging their homes and their kinship relations, their consumer purchases, and their schooling are in fact governed by a structuring logic of practice or *habitus*, that is, in turn, the product of historical and material forces beyond their control. Moreover, for Bourdieu, these choices, governed by a logic of which they are little aware, almost inevitably are *reproductive*, that is, they signify membership in a particular cultural or social group to others and to themselves, and in so signifying, they limit also the social and cultural parameters of individuals' aspirations.

This early work of Foucault and Bourdieu plays on the implicit deconstruction, of one of the most fundamental binaries of modernism: The distinction made in sixteenth-century philosopher Reneé Descartes' famous statement, "I think, therefore, I am"—that is, the distinction between the mind, or thoughts, and the body, or actions. However, in their work and in the work of other researchers and social theorists who focus on *practice*, or the underlying structures of a group's behavior, the internal process of thinking and the external process of doing or acting are conceived of as inseparably tied together: People form beliefs and attitudes in response to their physical, active experiences of the world, and their actions are seen to belie the underlying logic, or structure, of their cognition, far more so than any conscious explanation they might offer of their own behavior.

It is practice, then, that accounts for stability and continuity within cultural groups across time; yet it is this account of practice that also makes the prospect of social change or the chance for humans to exercise any creative agency in their own lives seem so limited, indeed, in the case of some theorists such as Jean Baudrillard (1988), almost hopeless. However, this is not the full story told by these theorists. Rather, I believe, they would assert that although regularity, predictability, and continuity are the primary structural goals of any functioning system of social meanings and practices, that those goals are achieved within a more particularized world in which the identities of individuals and the social arrangements in which they live are not nearly as normative or as clearly delineated as structuralist theory suggests.

Bourdieu, for example, in response to readings of his work as overly deterministic, has argued against this interpretation, pointing to the capacity of human beings (and in particular, for social scientists) to become more *reflexive* in their activities, that is, progressively more self-conscious of the consequences of their own behavior (1989). As a public discursive act, poststructural analysis—the act of demonstrating, or "outing," the false dichotomization of male v. female, the civilized v. the primitive mind, or the educated v. the ignorant—is also a potent form of structural resistance that, in time, can have a radical discursive effect.

The Brazilian educator Paulo Freire (1970) developed a theory of *critical pedagogy* grounded in a view of the world organized into economically driven binaries. From Marx, he drew an economically determined view of the social order, based on two classes: oppressors and the oppressed. From structural Marxists such as Althusser, he drew the image of the oppressed as largely unconscious of the ideology by which they were held in oppression; and from Gramsci, he drew the idea that education was the means by which ideology could be challenged. Freire's objective was to reverse the structurally oppressive effects of Northern (i.e. the United States) industrial capitalism and monetary policy on the people of economically struggling debtor nations such as Brazil. He believed that through pedagogical action aimed at producing *conscientization*, the oppressed could be helped not only to see the extent of the injustice they suffered but to find a way to take action to transform themselves and seek economic and political justice, that is, to achieve *praxis*, a condition in which one's actions, or practices, and theoretical vision (one's mind and body) are no longer opposed but in accord. Because of Freire's extensive use of binaries (oppressor/oppressed; North/South), his work has much in common with structuralism; yet, his awareness of the inequity that these binaries hold in place and refusal to accept these as given or inevitable marks him as proto-poststructuralist in his agenda.

Many other social theorists have looked for cultural spaces, both physical and discursive, in which individuals and marginalized social groups might find resources for resisting, and in time changing, the normative structures of societies. Foucault, for example, has described the historical existence of *heterotopic* spaces—spaces that are other to primary spaces such as homes or schools, such as gardens, museums, boarding schools, or even motel rooms—to which people escape in times of crisis to escape from discursive force and to restructure themselves (1986). Similarly, Pratt's concept of the *contact zone*—a temporal and physical space where two different groups might meet in creative production—has been taken up by some educational researchers in recent years (e.g. Ashley 2001), to imagine the culture of classrooms in "other" terms. And postcolonial theorist Arjun Appadurai (1996) has argued that accelerating advances in electronic technologies and air travel are providing images and ideas of material prosperity across the globe that produce imagined possibilities in far-flung places and new networks of association. These imaginaries transcend spatial boundaries and are revealing long-simmering tensions and contradictions within modernity's central political invention, the *nation-state.*

In his theory of the structure of rituals in both Western and tribal societies, Anglo-American anthropologist Victor Turner (1969) emphasized the importance of *liminality*, a temporal and spatial stage within the ritual process in which those who are in the process of transformation from child to adult, from being single to married, from uneducated to educated, or from a layperson to a minister or priest, for example, find themselves in a state of being characterized as *communitas*, an unstructured community in which all members are equal. Within communitas, individuals are temporarily freed from the norms and behaviors that structure either their former or their future social status, and from serious accountability for their actions as well. Liminality also brings them license to be critical of or even to mock their elders, and performatively to imagine a social order quite different from the society into which they are entering. Turner's theory has been applied to the analysis not only of religious rituals but in areas such as drama and theatre, and to the analysis of patterns of interaction between and among early adolescent students and their teachers (McLaren 1986) and school libarianship (Dressman 1997).

In a range of studies even more diverse than those inspired by Turner, popular culture theorist John Fiske (1987, 1989) has used poststructural principles to document the extent to which the sites and signs of mass popular culture, such as the movies, television, the wearing of blue jeans, and shopping malls, provide an almost endless smorgasbord of goods and services that people do not simply consume whole and in the ways intended by their producers, but instead read and often use in some very subversive ways. For example, many television quiz shows provide a setting in which what counts—and is rewarded—as "knowledge" is typically very different from what counts in school or within the culture as a whole as knowledge, such as the price of luxury items, or what one contestant may know about her or his partner's personal tastes and life history. These shows, according to Fiske, turn conventional, received valuations of academic capital ("book knowledge") upside down, as well as the entire ritual of examination and testing into a farce. They, thus, also offer a socially erosive challenge to the ideology of education itself and the binary it maintains between "high" academic culture (cultural capital) and what is popular or common and therefore of "low" worth.

Fiske's work provides a powerful frame for analyzing and understanding the popularity of websites such as MySpace.com (http://www.myspace.com), YouTube (http://www.youtube.com), or SecondLife (http://www.secondlife.com) as spaces in which anyone, anywhere (there's a computer and a high-speed Internet connection) can assert an identity of their own production, against the ideological marginalization they might suffer in the physical world as a result, for example, of race, class, gender, sexual orientation, or physical disability. Within educational research, Fiske's work resonates with recent studies in which adolescents who are disaffected by the tedium of schooling might find the resources within cyberspace to develop practices that challenge orthodox educational practices, particularly with respect to literacy. Knobel and Lankshear (2002), for example, characterized *zines*, a form of web-based publishing, as providing young women with a countercultural textual space in which to produce identities and exercise their literacy in ways that are far more engaging and self-directed than the sort of reading and writing activities authorized in school curricula. Similarly, in a recent presentation, Lemke (2007) described the opportunities afforded by websites such as FanFiction (http://www.fanfiction.net) to adolescent writers interested in "remixing"—rewriting, essentially—novels, manga (Japanese comics), television series, and movies, in ways that were more in line with their own tastes and personal interests.

Apart from social theorists strongly influenced by the work of Marx, Saussure, and Nietzsche, there are several other contemporary social theorists and schools of social theory whose work on practice has strong educational implications. John Dewey (1919; Dewey and Bentley 1949) was a philosopher and social reformer of the late nineteenth to mid-twentieth century whose views on educational and aesthetic practice continue to influence much scholarship today. Dewey was a founding member, along with Charles Sanders Peirce and William James, of a school of philosophy that has come to be known as American Pragmatism. Pragmatism (with a capital P) rejected the epistemological divide between objectivity and subjectivity, holding that although an objective reality might exist, human understanding of the world would always be filtered through subjective experience. This "middle of the road" position was a key component of Progressivism, a movement for social reform in which Dewey was a key player. Progressivists did not explain or excuse the social problems of industrial capitalism through the use of totalizing grand theories such as Marxism or Social Darwinism, whose proposed solutions were equally totalizing in their implications. Instead, they pressed for a program of reform of specific institutions, such as schools, that was grounded in a practice of careful consideration of the short- and long-term consequences of actions, not only for individuals within those institutions, but for society as a whole.

Thus, although Pragmatism and its action-oriented movement, Progressivism, shared a strong sense of outrage with Marxism over the consequences of industrial capitalism, their response to these ills was more influenced by a Darwinian, ecological, perspective on the mutual interdependence of (the human) species and the physical and social environment over time. This relationship is best captured in Dewey's last book (Dewey and Bentley 1949), in which he characterizes human exchange, both socially and with physical objects, as *transactional*. By this term, Dewey meant to note that in acting *on* the world, the world—be it social or physical—acts on the actor, and that a single action, when viewed in its full context, can be seen to have been the consequence of, and to have consequences for, a long chain of similar past and future social and physical exchanges, or transactional experiences.

Dewey's concept of human experience in transactional terms has broad implications for the reform of educational practice. For example, it mandates a view of education as an experiential activity, in which human beings engage in activities that are simultaneously physical, intellectual, and social, and for a view of education and curriculum tied closely to the development of society itself. It also implies a close relationship between research and practice, but not a relationship that is so locally focused that either the long-term or the broader societal consequences of research or practice are ignored. Finally, it has significant implications for analyzing the ways in which students, teachers, and the public at large come in contact with and make sense of artistic works, scientific practice and knowledge, and history, politics, and culture.

Dewey's views on education as a social process are sometimes associated with Social Constructivism and Activity Theory, two schools of learning theory that ground their theoretical origins in Cultural-Historical Psychology, which was founded by Soviet psychologist Lev Vygotsky and his contemporaries Alexi Leont'ev and Alexander Luria in the 1930s (see also Wertsch 1985). As discussed earlier in this chapter, Vygotsky's view of human learning was grounded in Marxist principles of dialectical materialism. Social Constructivism views learning in almost exclusively social terms, and relies largely on Vygotsky's concept of the Zone of Proximal Development, a social-temporal space in which a learner, through interactions with more knowledgeable others, is led to solve a problem and thus acquire new skills and knowledge. However, in actual practice, Social Constructivism has largely lost the broader framework of Marxist social and political critique that motivated Vygotsky's original work.

## Strategies for reading

I want to end this chapter by returning to the discussion with which it began, about the challenges that readers outside the discourses of social theory face when they first try to "enter the conversation," as my former teacher, Linda Brodkey, once put it. As befits a discourse intended to counter the orthodox linearity and sometimes forced symmetry of modernism, contemporary social theory is an ill-structured, historically and discursively tangled, and loosely ordered network of counterintuitive ideas and strategies, whose ultimate aim is not to deconstruct or tear down the social order as some have claimed, but to re-imagine and re-figure the world in more equitable and culturally engaging terms. Social theory would therefore seem to hold enormous potential as a tool for seeing educational problems anew, if only it weren't so complex and many of its texts were not so impenetrable. In addition, I want to warn readers that the presentation of many of its major concepts and theorists in this chapter hardly scratches the surface of the literature. Indeed, I worry that I may have performed readers a disservice by presenting a more coherent and ordered portrait of social theory than is the case, and so have provided a false sense of understanding.

What can be done about this? You might try to take a university course, hoping that the instructor will be a patient and well-prepared tutor and guide who will carefully select and structure a range of theorists and texts. My own experience of these courses, however, has been that instructors often try to mimic the same obscurity and complexity in their language as many social theorists, and that the texts they select are often idiosyncratic. Or, you could join a reading group and fumble around with others, typically with similar effect. In the end, I am afraid that reading social theory is more likely to be primarily a solitary journey, and one whose rewards will come over time.

There are, however, some strategies for making that journey easier and more productive. First, nearly all the theorists discussed in this chapter understand human social behavior as patterned and historically constructed, place as much if not more emphasis on external, social factors than on individual, psychological difference, and see human behavior as motivated by material and historical, rather than spiritual, forces. Keeping this perspective in mind and actively trying to imagine the questions and issues that it raises, for example, in explaining the origins of language, may help a reader to understand the purpose behind a theoretical argument.

Second, as a starting place for educational researchers, it can be very useful to locate published studies on a topic of interest that make substantial use of one or more social theorists, to see how these researchers explain the social theory they are using and its implications for their work.

However, although reading others' work is a good place to start, I would not advise assuming that the way in which a particular study uses social theory is necessarily comprehensive or accurate. Some researchers may borrow terms or general ideas from the body of a social theorist's work uncritically or use some concepts in ways that actually contradict basic principles of the theory from which the term was taken. English literature educator Louise Rosenblatt's (1978) (mis)appropriation of John Dewey's concept of transaction is one such example (see Dressman and Webster 2001; Dressman 2004). It may be a more useful strategy to read several research studies on different topics that all use the same social theoretical resources, to compare and contrast different researchers' readings and uses of theory, and then to read the original texts that are referenced in the studies. This strategy may provide a clearer understanding of the social theorist's work and its potential application to an educational problem.

Third, beyond reading the work of other researchers, it is imperative to read the original writings of social theorists, and if they prove confusing, to look for support from commentaries and other secondary works. One quick and generally (although not always) accurate source of background information is the Internet. Wikipedia (http://www.wikipedia.org) is a user-written and user-maintained, free online encyclopedia that provides basic background information and a bibliography for nearly every social theorist mentioned in this chapter. Entries on Marxism and its variants are particularly well-developed and well-organized on this website. The entries also introduce the major concepts and terms used by individual theorists and schools of theory, and nearly all of these are hyperlinked. A second useful online resource is The Internet Encyclopedia of Philosophy (http://www.iep .utm.edu), which provides an alphabetical index and brief summary of the basic concepts of nearly every major contemporary and historical Western philosopher, along with multiple links to other websites for each listing.

A third source of information is through general search engines, such as Google.com (http://www.google.com), and Altavista.com. Many university professors and individuals around the world provide "fan sites" for their favorite philosophers and social theorists, which include very readable, if sometimes biased, summaries of their work and its implications, along with links to other sites and, in some cases, downloadable copies of primary texts. One such site devoted to Jacques Derrida can be found at (http://www.lichtensteiger.de/derridalinks.html). This site is essentially a long list of links to other sites on Derrida. Another interesting site is SaussureScape (http://www.sou.edu/English/IDTC/Projects/Saussure/saussrex.htm), an interactive site dedicated to expanding on the work of Ferdinand de Saussure. A final example is Marxists Internet Archive (http://www.marxists.org), an extremely well-developed resource for all Marxist things. Again, while these resources are a very useful source of basic information about many different schools of social theory, they are no substitute for reading the original work, nor should any single site be trusted to provide the truth about a social theorist or school of theory. There is no Truth! So, triangulate, compare and contrast, and understanding will grow by and by.

A wide range of books that provide both introductory overviews and introductory commentary to the work of nearly every major social theorist are also available. One of the most comprehensive and readable introductions currently available is *Postmodern Theory: Critical Interrogations* (1991), by Steven Best and Douglas Kellner. The book presents a lively recounting of structuralism and poststructural theory, from Lévi-Strauss through Foucault, Deleuze and Guattari, feminist poststructuralism, and the Frankfurt School of critical theory in very conversational, at times almost gossipy, terms. A subsequent volume by the same authors, *The Postmodern Turn* (Best and Kellner 1997), provides an overview of recent applications of postmodern theory in areas such as popular culture studies, the arts, and the sociology of science.

There are also multiple commentaries devoted to the work of individual theorists and schools of theory. The Routledge series, *Key Sociologists* presents critical introductions to the work of several major theorists, including Pierre Bourdieu (Jenkins 2002), Michel Foucault (Smart 2002), and Karl Marx (Worsley 2002). Another very useful series published by Routledge is *New Accents*, which includes several very authoritative commentaries on individual theorists, including Mikhail Bakhtin (*Dialogism: Bakhtin and His World*, Holquist 2002), and Derrida (*Deconstruction: Theory and Practice,* Norris 2002). The work of other major theorists mentioned in this chapter, such as Vygotsky and Gee, is more readable; however, readers interested in the full implications of Vygotsky's work for education should consult James Wertsch's classic volume, *Vygotsky and the Social Formation of Mind* (1985).

Another reading strategy for particularly difficult authors is to read their biographies. It helps greatly, for example, when reading Foucault's historical critique of the discourses of madness and disease, to know that Foucault was gay and estranged from his physician father, who wanted Foucault to join him in his practice, or when struggling through *The Order of Things* (Foucault 1994), to read David Macey's (1993) biographical account of its writing. Similarly, Ray Monk's biography, *Ludwig Wittgenstein: The Duty of Genius* (1990), provides a powerful introduction to the development of Wittgenstein's work over time, and makes a fine companion to *Philosophical Investigations* (Wittgenstein 1953).

A final and very critical strategy is to reconsider what it popularly means to read a text in the early twenty-first century. Our popular habits of reading have been shaped by a culture in which people have become accustomed to being "sold" on the consumption of goods through promises of convenience and ease. The texts of everyday living, such as newspapers, magazines, best-selling novels, and self-help books (including this book, to some extent) are all written in language that is (deceptively, some would say) transparent and that typically needs no more than one passage through for its (intended) meaning(s) to be extracted.

In making this point I do not mean to suggest, in the style of some moralizing right-wing pundit, that we have all become intellectually lazy and that Western civilization is in danger of going to hell because of its reading habits. Rather, my point is that if readers reflected on the extent to which those habits have been culturally shaped, then an adjustment of them and in the ways that the texts of social theory are approached might seem more reasonable. Readers might also not feel so frustrated or so cheated or even so incompetent when they encounter a sentence like the one from Bourdieu's (1990) *The Logic of Practice* that I quoted at the beginning of this chapter. They might, instead, approach it more slowly. They might pause and return to it, revisiting and rereading it within its full textual context over multiple occasions, after consulting one or more secondary commentaries on Bourdieu's concept of *habitus* and reading other research studies to see how the term is used in them. Finally, they would decide for themselves whether the concept is meaningful, that is, whether, based on their own reasoning and experience, it justifiably and usefully accounts for an element of social reality. Then they would be reading and *participating in* the discourses social theory as their authors intended: As a series of conversations filled with ideas and reasoning processes that are necessarily counterintuitive and challenging, but that hold the promise of fresh and generative insights into the problems of the modern world.

# Chapter 2

# Social theory and the rhetoric of educational research

## Introduction

Over the last 50 years, an enormous philosophical literature has accumulated on the topic of what makes research practices truly "scientific." Behind that literature are other more anxiety-ridden questions that give this topic great cultural value and discursive energy. They are, simply: How do we ever know anything for sure? How can we trust what we know? And, ultimately, is there an objective reality that human beings can discover, or not?

These questions have also dogged the practices of educational research since it became a major field of study, around the same time that the literature on the nature of science also began to expand. At first, the answer to these questions within educational research was relatively straightforward and was grounded in a view of scientific activity as exclusively experimental, if not *positivistic*, or objectivist in an absolute sense. This view assumed that human social behavior was governed by principles similar to those of the physical and biological world, that is, that there were general structures, or patterns, to human behavior that applied across specific cultures and other social groups. Moreover, this view assumed that these patterns were discoverable through procedures that isolated discreet variables and that "controlled" for the possibility that their identification and measurement were biased by errors of human perception or judgment. In other words, educational research assumed that as long as one's methods were "clean" and took into account any possible "validity threats," or conceivable human bias, then one's findings could be trusted as valid and applicable, at least to the part of the general population that one was studying. Over multiple experiments, an increasing number of discreet variables and their interrelations, or interactions, would also be discovered, so that a general model of some aspect of human behavior—reading comprehension, for example, or mathematical problem solving—would be built up. Then researchers would know how these processes worked, and their findings could be rationally applied to the development of better educational practices and policies.

## The example of phonemic/phonological awareness research

As an illustration of some of the serious problems this view of research creates when it is applied to educational questions, let me present findings from an analysis I performed a few years ago of experimental research and its implications on an topic in early reading called *phonemic* (or sometimes *phonological*) *awareness* (Dressman 1999). For much of the twentieth century, a "Great Debate" (Adams 1990) had raged within the field of reading research over the "best" way to teach young children to read. One side argued that a phonics-based method, in which children were taught to recognize words by blending together the sounds represented by combinations of letters in a word was the most efficient and reliable approach for all children. The other side argued that a word-based (and later, through much extension and theorizing, a "whole-language") approach, in which children were taught to use some phonics in combination with a range of other cues such as context, word shape, and memorization of sight words, was more advantageous in the long term. In the 1960s, the US federal government funded a massive study to compare the difference between these two methods, but results were mixed and regarded as inconclusive by many researchers and practitioners, and so the debate raged on.

Then, in the 1980s, a new line of experimental research seemed to offer significant evidence in support of the phonics method. Researchers studying phonemic/phonological awareness (PPA), which is the ability of the speakers of a language to isolate and identify the individual sounds of a spoken word (to be able to know there are three sounds in /cat/, for example, and to be able to identify each), noted a strong association, or correlation, between the phonemic awareness of young children, aged 3–5, and their later success in learning to read. The more proficient children were in segmenting and identifying the individual phonemes, or sounds, of words, the more quickly and easily they grasped the *alphabetic principle* that individual written letters represented individual sounds, and the more quickly they learned to decode and read whole words and sentences. Later research seemed to establish that a causal relationship existed between PPA and reading achievement. It was reasoned, therefore, that if children could be taught to become more phonemically/phonologically aware, they would have a greater chance of learning to read, or at least to decode written language—that is, to turn written words into speech. Since PPA seemed more congruent in principle with phonics-based rather than whole-word/language-based reading methods, it was also reasoned that the research evidence provided a sound justification for using phonics-based methods of reading instruction.

Not one but many separate experimental studies all seemed to corroborate and extend this line of reasoning. And since strict experimental procedures had been followed and the conclusions seemed almost to emerge self-evidently from the data, it also seemed reasonable to conclude that the need for direct instruction in PPA in preschools and kindergartens and later for phonics-based reading instruction had been scientifically established as fact.

But there were a few problems with this entire line of research and its conclusions. For example, PPA research was based on a definition of a phoneme that was analogous to the definition of a chemical element, that is, as an irreducible, tangible entity that combined with other similar elements to form a more complex compound (a word, for example, and in even greater complexity, a sentence). The question of whether phonemes exist at all is a point of dispute within phonological theory and research, however, because acoustic studies of language show that when we speak we do not pronounce individual sounds within words; instead, they tend to slide together and interact with each other based on their contiguity. Try making the /p/ sound, for example, in isolation. Then, say "pea," "beep," and "rupture." Is the /p/ in each instance the same sound, exactly? Okay, you say: it's a little different in each word. But you recognize it as the same sound, so it's a phoneme, right? It's *real*, right?

Yes, it's real; but it's not natural, as PPA researchers assumed. Instead, it's completely cultural; and moreover, the ability to distinguish among the individual sounds of a spoken word is highly dependent not only on the exercise being carried out in one's own language, but, because of phonological variation within languages, on one's own dialect. Ask a British speaker of English, for example, how many sounds and syllables there are in the word, "schedule" (*shed-djoo-ull*); then ask an American (*sked-djul*). Or, have you ever found yourself utterly frustrated and embarrassed because you couldn't pronounce a word from a foreign language, such as the name of a person or a place, to a foreign speaker's satisfaction, no matter how hard you tried? We are conditioned by our own speech communities to recognize some sounds as phonemes and either not to recognize or to hear others differently. We are, therefore, a great deal more phonemically/phonologically aware of our home dialect of our own native language than we are of other dialects and most certainly of other languages.

The influence of dialect and native v. non-native language ability would therefore seem to offer a clear explanation for another of these studies' findings: That linguistic minority children (children who did not speak English at home, or who came from communities that spoke a dialect different from the researchers) consistently scored lower on measures of PPA than did children from linguistic majority homes who spoke the normative dialect of English for the study. Yet, there was no recognition of the cultural, sociolinguistic basis of PPA in any of the major research studies that I reviewed for my (1999) analysis. Although the linguistic backgrounds of the subjects (the children) were identified, no mention was made of the linguistic backgrounds of the researchers themselves. However, their names and professional backgrounds strongly suggested that they were nearly all White and members of professional language communities. Imagine four- and five-year-olds from relatively closed and often impoverished communities being individually asked to analyze the sounds in words spoken to them by White adults who were largely strangers and who spoke a language or dialect of English different from their own, and the implications of the phonemic/phonological mismatch between tester and tested would seem obvious.

If not in terms of linguistic and dialectical variance, how did researchers explain differences in their measures of PPA for linguistically normative and linguistic minority children? Most of the original research studies did not speculate on the causes of their findings. However, in a separate major review of the evidence, Marilyn Adams (1990: 87) suggested that it was because the parents of children who tested poorly for PPA did not have the same values or engage in the same pre-literacy practices as more successful children. One of the original researchers, Keith Stanovich, in an article with a biblical allusion in its title, "Matthew Effects in Reading: Some Consequences of Individual Differences in the Acquisition of Literacy" (after a verse from Book of Matthew supporting the adage that "the rich get richer, and the poor get poorer"), argued that the parental "genotypes" (1986: 383) of children with low measures of PPA were inferior to those of higher performing children. Much like Herbert Spencer in the nineteenth century, Stanovich drew on Darwin's theory of natural selection to argue that the superior school achievement of children from middle-class homes was due to the genetic superiority of middle-class families, as evidenced by home literacy behaviors that produced superior academic performance in school.

From their publication in 1986 and 1990 and continuing well after my analysis was published in 1999, "Matthew Effects" and *Beginning to Read* were read uncritically, as arguments grounded in scientific evidence whose methodology rendered their findings and conclusions indisputable. They were foundational in the reform of reading education policy in both California and Texas in the mid-1990s and influenced US federal educational policy during both the Clinton and Bush administrations. Yet, it is also clear that regardless of their experimental methodology, the conceptualization of PPA itself was fraught with naive and false assumptions about phonology and linguistics that led to egregiously racist and classist interpretations of findings that, in turn, supported ill-conceived and bigoted educational policies and practices.

## Two axioms

The example of PPA research illustrates the first axiom of educational (or, for that matter, any kind or method of) research in this book: *Data never speak for themselves.* At every stage, from the conceptualization of a problem or a question to the design of a study, through data collection and analysis to interpretation and the writing up of findings, unexamined assumptions, personal and cultural biases, and sometimes even unacknowledged bigotry, intrude, to lesser or greater extent on researchers' sense-making processes. It is in the nature of inquiry itself—in the condition of not knowing something *for sure* but going ahead and doing one's best to find it out anyway, *because of the human difference that knowledge will make*—that misunderstandings almost inevitably occur and mistakes of judgment are made. Values and the fact that all prior knowledge is only partial always affect the production of what counts as knowledge.

This axiom is valid wherever research has a social and normative dimension, regardless of whether the questions asked concern theoretical physics (witness Einstein's famous dismissal of quantum mechanics, "God does not play dice with the universe"), biological studies of sexual difference and human behavior (Longino 1990), or the social sciences, but more obviously so in the latter, where social consequences are likely to be more direct and immediate. Researchers very often tend to find what they are looking for. Most researchers who studied PPA, in the present example, were predisposed to favor a phonics-based approach to reading; and PPA research can largely be read as a quest to find a causal link between spoken, "natural" language and print literacy that would provide hard "proof" of the efficacy of phonics-based reading instruction.

It would be unfair and completely inaccurate, however, to charge PPA researchers with being deliberately racist, classist, or in any way deceptive or unethical in their research practices. To the contrary, I know personally that many of these individuals were quite liberal in terms of their social and political philosophies and positions, and quite committed to issues of social justice in their work. Reading their research reports, it is very clear that their research was driven by a deep desire to find a better way to teach young children of all backgrounds how to read, and that they believed that applying the procedures and logic of hard experimental science were key to achieving that goal. When I first presented my analysis of PPA research to several reading researchers in the field, they were shocked; they simply hadn't noticed the implications of Stanovich's argument, and hadn't thought at all about the issues of dialectical variation I had raised. They fully believed that the rationality of the scientific method meant that the data *had* spoken for themselves in this instance, and that the evidence was completely convincing of the conclusions they had drawn. The honesty and forthrightness with which they made their claims only underscores the point made by multiple recent philosophers of science: That being fully "scientific" in one's research practices must involve a great deal more than following a particular method of inquiry to the letter (Bauer 1994; Feyerabend 1993; Shapin 1996). It must also involve extreme skepticism and self-questioning at every step of the process, a candid appraisal of the theories, both formal and informal, that support one's reasoning, and the humility to admit that all knowledge is ultimately tentative and partial.

The case of PPA research is also illustrative of a second axiom in this book: *Doing educational research is a rhetorical activity.* Although the term *rhetorical* in common parlance often implies trickery, or the attempt to persuade readers or listeners through the use of inflammatory or emotionally charged language rather than through reason, in ancient times and in contemporary academic use—and as I use it here—it refers to techniques and practices for making "good" (i.e. convincing) arguments. By this definition, and drawing on principles of speech act theory (Austin 1975) and Habermas's (1984) Theory of Communicative Action, nearly every form of extended language use, be it spoken or written, is a rhetorical activity. A front-page story in a newspaper, for example, is rhetorically driven in its efforts to convince readers of the factuality and trustworthiness of the information and its "objective" reporting of those facts. A letter to home from a soldier at war is an attempt to persuade loved ones that all is well. Novels use language to draw readers into fictional worlds and to persuade them of the plausibility of relationships and events; poems aim to move readers to emotional response and aesthetic delight. And as I write this chapter I find myself continually making decisions about topic, word choice, sentence structure, and paragraph order, all in an attempt to lead an imagined reader to believe that my ideas about educational research are authoritative, sensible, and worth putting into practice. Beyond the making of simple lists, it seems that writing is always about persuading a potential reader of the validity and worth of information and ideas. There is nothing amiss or unusual about rhetorical activity, it would seem; in fact, one might argue that without it communication would be nearly impossible.

But if this is so, why bother to mention it at all? The reason is that different genres of text conventionally emphasize different features of writing to influence readers. In traditional educational research, the tendency has been to emphasize the transparency of a study's methods, as a means of influencing readers to believe that its findings are valid—in other words, that the data do, in fact, speak for themselves.

However, the case of PPA research demonstrates the folly of this claim. Methodologically, the experimental designs and statistical analyses undertaken across multiple studies of PPA were sound. It was the inadequate conceptualization and definition of one of the basic elements of the studies—the phoneme—in combination with later researchers' and authors' unexamined beliefs about the backgrounds of linguistic minorities that led to questionable conclusions that supported poor policy decisions. It seems that to take the position that one's methods validate one's research—that methodology can or will lead to self-evident conclusions about a phenomenon—without a broader examination of all the assumptions one makes about a phenomenon, is to depend on false reasoning, and to engage in a rhetorical practice that may deceive both oneself and others. And if this were the case for research that was apparently rational and scientific in its procedures, it would be even more so for studies that were more qualitative and ethnographic, in which data collection did not occur under controlled conditions and that may very well have been opportunistic and uneven, and in which the judgment and beliefs of the researcher figured into the project at every turn.

This is a maddening problem. If data never speak for themselves, if it requires a priori, or pre-existing, intellectual and practical structures to give them meaning, which in turn support the linguistic, rhetorical conventions that give it force, or influence, in the world, but those intellectual and practical structures are themselves fraught with assumptions that may be false or not fit the circumstances of the question being asked, what chance is there of producing knowledge that is accurate, or of acting on knowledge without fear that a mistake will be made whose consequences are unforeseen?

## Tensions within research approaches

This is a question that challenges the hard sciences philosophically, but the social sciences and educational research in a far more constant way, and with more direct and severe political and social consequences. Its lack of resolution in these latter fields has reduced both the utility and the status of social science and educational research. In the United States, at least, it has led to the formation of methodological/epistemological camps within educational research, each of which has its own approach to dealing with this question. Experimental and quasi-experimental researchers, for instance, typically ignore or deny that there is a problem such as the one I have described here, claiming that the use of "scientific methods" assures the production of objective, valid, and generalizable research findings.

Although researchers who use qualitative and ethnographic methods are typically far more cognizant and concerned about these issues, their responses are diverse and, as I will argue, are also problematic in a number of ways. Researchers in the *grounded theory* camp (Glaser and Strauss 1967) would analyze data collected in the form of interviews, observational notes, and artifacts using low-inference coding practices to identify recurring themes, or patterns of relations, across and within data sources. Like experimentalists, users of grounded theory argue that findings "emerge" or are "discovered" or "revealed," rather than constructed through this process, and that the low level of inference, that is, of personal involvement, in the coding process assures that the findings are more or less objective and that anyone else who analyzed the data would find essentially the same themes. Like experimentalists also, users of grounded theory aim to find an underlying essence, or general pattern of relations, that bears comparison to a broader population beyond the sample that was studied.

Other qualitative approaches such as *case study* (Stake 1995) and *naturalistic inquiry* (Lincoln and Guba 1985) use methods of analysis similar to grounded theory, but emphasize the peculiarities of the particular situation and participants to a greater extent. Like grounded theory, these approaches aim to produce a low-inference, objective description of a local situation, but they avoid questions of the applicability of findings to other settings by denying generalizability and depend, instead, on *member checks* (presenting one's findings to participants to confirm the accuracy of data interpretation) as a way of establishing the internal validity of findings. Indeed, one of the central tenets of these approaches is that the differences within populations and settings are far more salient and significant than any generalities that may be discerned.

A third group of qualitative, ethnographic approaches deals with issues of assumptive bias and generalizability by embracing these, within local contexts, as not only inevitable but perhaps even desirable. *Interpretive ethnography* (Denzin 1996), *action* and *teacher research* (Cochran-Smith and Lytle 1992), and *new ethnography* (Goodall 2000) completely reject any claims of objectivity, arguing, instead, that the perspective of the researcher is not only an inevitable but a very useful aspect of inquiry and problem solving, and that *thick description* (Geertz 2000) of specific instances is more valid and reveals more about the full complexities of human social life than does any general description of a phenomena whose claims of objectivity and generalizability are always suspect.

Although each of these qualitative and ethnographic approaches offers a response to questions of validity in social science and educational research, none fully resolves them. The use of "low-inference" codes in grounded theory, for example, provides no more assurance that unforeseen bias or assumptions will influence findings than in the case of PPA research. Case study and naturalistic inquiry methods avoid questions of the general validity of their findings and focus instead on generating accounts that are internally valid, "true" descriptions within discreet settings; but in the process they significantly reduce the rhetorical power of their findings, as well as fail to account for the possibility that researchers and participants could be mutually unaware of the influence of hidden (and inaccurate) assumptions. Interpretive ethnography, action and teacher research, and new, confessional, ethnographic approaches at times seem to take an almost defiant stance toward issues of validity and generalizability, but they do so at the expense of an even greater reduction in their rhetorical influence on policy and general practice. They also open themselves to the charge that they are little more than self-indulgent and solipsistic processes whose ultimate consequence may likely be the reproduction of the status quo (Dressman 1998).

Moreover, I will argue that advocates in the last two groups of qualitative and ethnographic approaches are not being completely accurate, either with themselves or with others, when they state that their methods are not intended to produce generalizable findings. If this were the case, then every published case study and naturalistic report would have to be written—and read—as completely fresh and new, and understood without reference to the reader or writer's prior knowledge or experience of people or situations. And yet, the narratives of these studies make routine use of conventional categories of race, class, gender, and setting, categories that invoke in readers very conventional, even stereotypical meanings. The characterization of a student as "Latino" in the United States, for example, invokes multiple connotations: Of limited English proficiency, of possible undocumented immigrant status, of low socioeconomic status, and of problematic home–school relations. Whether accurate or not, these are all hidden generalities, and they invite readers to relate the particular individual or situation under discussion to these general categories as well. In addition, the strong narrative style of most of these accounts also has the effect of pulling a reader into the situation, and of *interpellating*, or hailing, that reader in Althusserian terms (Althusser 1971), as a character—most probably the researcher-narrator—within the story, and inviting comparison between the reader's experience and situation and the situation in the text. In these ways, the authors of qualitative and ethnographic research studies overtly renounce the generalizability of their findings even as they covertly instruct their readers to produce generalities within the situations they describe.

This epistemological impasse and the tension it generates among research approaches in the social sciences and educational research was exacerbated in the United States during the Bush administration, which sided with experimentalists and against qualitative and ethnographic research. One consequence was the placement of tight restrictions that effectively eliminated research proposals from consideration for federal funding that were not experimental or quasi-experimental; another was the instigation of a purge of non-experimental research studies from federal research archives and databases. Yet, despite these developments, the use of qualitative and ethnographic approaches to educational research since the 1980s has continued to increase. For example, in a recent survey of trends in literacy research within three major US journals (Dressman 2007), I found that whereas before 1990 the overwhelming majority of studies in the journals were experimental or quasi-experimental in their approach, after 1990 and with increasing frequency through 2003, the overwhelming majority were qualitative and ethnographic. While that trend has reached a plateau since 2003, it remains the case that the overwhelming majority of literacy research published today is qualitative, both methodologically and epistemologically.

A greater, more global, and longer lasting scholarly consequence of this impasse, however, may be the atomization of the knowledge base about social and educational phenomena. On the one hand, the gradual erosion of any claims of generalizability with regard to what is known or not known about education and its replacement with a number of small, self-contained studies as numerous as the stars in the sky may signal the increasing democratization of educational research and its discourses. It may also help to dissipate the power of educational forces that, after Foucault (1977) and many other continental philosophers, depend on the generalizability of their knowledge claims to exercise authority and control in schools and in spheres of policy making.

On the other hand, like the stars in the sky, the atomization of educational research may not provide the field with sufficient illumination for educators and policy makers to see issues clearly or formulate sound general policy. Moreover, in the absence of clear connections or relations among studies, the tendency to find connections among studies in idiosyncratic ways that are misleading or that lead to popular and uncritical acceptance of generalities also remains very possible. In other words, a research trend that may seem to realize the democratization of research and redistribution of power relations within education may just as possibly lead to a loss of cohesion and utility within educational discourse, and impede progress in educational policy and practice across local, national, and perhaps global levels.

## Taking a different approach

These long-standing epistemological, methodological, and recently political challenges within social science and educational research may appear daunting, especially to researchers in the early stages of their careers. I am going to argue in the remainder of this and the next chapters, however, that the situation is not completely as intractable as this discussion paints it, although the adjustment that I propose requires a rather radical shift in research practice and, as Pierre Bourdieu (1990) might say, in the *dispositions* that structure the planning, implementation, and writing up of a research study. The major dispositional shift is in researchers' responses to the two axioms I have discussed, away from seeing these conditions as hindrances to the validation of their practices—that is, as problems to be solved—and toward the embrace of their implications, or as the very means to producing general and valid, but by no means absolute or complete, bodies of knowledge within the social sciences and education.

For example, there is a need to reread the axiom that *data never speak for themselves* not as an admission that human bias always creeps into the research process, but as an affirmation of data's embeddedness within the social structures of language, discourse, meaning, and practice. Data are not discrete things, but networks of associations that have been systematically lifted out of the larger, thicker, historically constructed web of associations that structures our sense of the world. They do not *speak* at all, but have meaning projected out of them through the lens of a researcher's sense, be it implicit or explicit, of how the world operates. Where that sense is implicit, or where it is explicit—where it is formally stated and named as a *theory*—and tacitly accepted or even adhered to as a fact, it will tend to project an interpretation that is bent to fit the contours of the researcher's pre-existing sense of the world. But where that sense is articulated in formal, theoretical terms that are themselves understood as problematic and tentative, often in unforeseen ways, then data can have, after Latour (2005), some *agency*. As agents, data can also have some independent capacity for surprising researchers, for causing them to see a lack of fit between what they expected and what the data suggest, and for forming new or modified networks of associations that better account for not only the phenomenon under investigation but that help to restructure researchers' theoretical sense of the world.

Since they are explicit and were consciously constructed as critiques of modern logic, or sensibilities, the social theories discussed in the Introduction and Chapter One of this book offer extraordinary possibilities for the realization of the latter scenario above over the former. Imagine, for example, the difference that some grounding in Saussurean linguistics or Gee's sociolinguistics or Bourdieu's theory of social reproduction could have made in the interpretation of PPA research. But let me also be clear here: I am not suggesting that Saussure or Gee or Bourdieu or any social theory represents a stronger set of truths than a researcher's common sense or less socially motivated theory. Rather, social theory offers a sense of the world that is different from what is typically presumed, and so it provides a context for new associations and meanings to be formed from data. Nor do I mean to suggest that social theory is not itself problematic or tentative; on the contrary, an uncritical adherence to its tenets would be just as likely to bend data to fit its contours as would any other theoretical framework.

Second, there is a need to shift the interpretation of the axiom that *research is a rhetorical activity* away from the suggestion that persuasion requires writers to bend truths toward the understanding that the construction of good arguments—ones that hold up under the scrutiny of alternative perspectives and interpretations—is critical to the construction of new knowledge. Moreover, characterizing research as a rhetorical activity implies that the making of good arguments does not begin where the research process ends, but that the making of good arguments drives the entire research process, from conceptualization to design to data collection, analysis, and interpretation. By this I do not mean to suggest, however, that research should be a process in which one begins by deciding on the argument one wants to make and then contrives a process that will produce data that "speak for themselves" in support of the argument one wanted to make. Nor do I mean to imply that one needs to "pick" a social theory and then organize one's research around it. Rather, I mean that the point of doing research is to gather evidence to make an argument about what *is* and what *should be*, and that this requires that social science and educational research begin with the disposition to view the topic to be studied as an inherently social phenomenon, embedded within a broad network of language, discourse, meaning, and practice that must be taken into account at each stage of the project.

Finally, the making of good arguments about social and educational phenomena requires researchers to take an implicitly Habermasian (Habermas 1984) perspective regarding the social, rhetorical work that the construction of a good argument can perform in the world. Habermas's Theory of Communicative Action provides a compelling and well-developed argument that the truth claims of any argument can be determined to be valid or invalid by speakers through open, rational discourse. This is because of the *communicative competence*, or capacity of speakers to understand each other through a sharing of tacit rules of discursive exchange and *intersubjectivity* (the ability to grasp another person's point of view and reasoning processes) within a context of free and open, non-coercive speech (what Habermas terms an *ideal speech situation*), which we all inherently possess as the vested members of a discourse community. In a Habermasian scenario, a good argument is one that is made in public, and that is validated within in a forum that allows for open inspection and questioning of reasoning processes from a variety of perspectives. Moreover, there is an implicit distinction to be made in the criteria by which the argument's validity is judged, depending on whether the argument is about an issue that is physical/objective, normative/evaluative, or subjective in its orientation. In the case of educational research, this typically involves a coordination of criteria among questions of physical/objective validity (i.e. about the existence of a phenomenon and the accuracy of its described relations) and questions of normative/evaluative validity (i.e. about the conceptualization and interpretation of issues' social implications). Habermas's argument is that through this process sound reasoning is distinguished from weak or deceptive reasoning, sound knowledge is produced, and progress is made.

## Social theory and the making of good arguments: four examples

Practically, then, if data never speak for themselves and if research is a rhetorical activity, how are good arguments made? What are their elements, what is their syntax, or their grammar, and within them, what part does or can social theory play? To illustrate the range of ways in which social theory is currently used within educational research arguments, I present an analysis of the central arguments of four articles published in recent issues of major Anglophone educational journals. By *central arguments*, I mean the claims that researchers make in their overall conceptualization of the research project, the reasoning behind their methods of data collection and analysis, the interpretations they apply to their findings, and the explicit or implicit claims for the rightness of the claims made within the published report. These are the arguments that constitute the core meanings to be taken from any published research report.

### Toulmin's model of argumentation

The model of argumentation proposed by Stephen Toulmin in *The Uses of Argument* (1958) offers one way of framing an analysis of the differing ways in which social theories contribute to the making of arguments in educational research. Toulmin began his analysis by noting that in everyday life speakers typically assume that arguments consist of two elements, a statement of fact, or a *datum*, which produces or supports an equally obvious conclusion, or *claim*, as in the proposition, "Storm clouds are gathering; it looks like rain." Closer inspection of the relation of the datum to the claim, even in this very simple instance, shows that relationship to be supported by an intervening set of assumptions about meteorological conditions and weather patterns. Toulmin termed these intervening assumptions the *warrant* of a propositional statement, and he argued that all such statements, or *illocutionary acts* (statements that mean to advance a claim persuasively) contain at least one warrant. Warrants, in turn, are either implicitly or explicitly supported by evidence of their own, which he termed *backing*. Thus, the statement above is warranted by the assumption that dark clouds precede rainfall, which in turn is backed by meteorological records and the prior experiences of the speaker with rainy weather.

But there are also instances in which the propositional content of a statement is only contingent—that is, dependent on additional factors. For example, the clouds may blow over, or other conditions, such as the temperature or insufficient moisture, may prevent rain from falling, or it may rain but only very little. Toulmin termed such intervening circumstances *qualifiers*, since they act to limit, or qualify, the applicability of a proposition's claims within specified contexts or situations. He also noted that many times a qualifier may in turn be contradicted, or as he termed it, *rebutted*. Thus, since dark clouds are gathering (the datum) and this is typically a precondition of precipitation (the warrant), at least from past observations of rainy conditions (the backing) it's going to rain (the claim)—perhaps not here or very much (the qualifier), but those clouds will produce rain somewhere (the rebuttal).

However, it is important to note that for Toulmin's model to "work," all its elements are not required to be explicit. In everyday speech contexts, people's statements are seldom so fully developed. Rather than explore all the contingencies and reasons behind the likelihood of rain, speakers typically cut to the quick and assume that the warrants and qualifiers of an argument are understood, and, in a fully developed argument, can be supplied if the claim is challenged.

Toulmin's greatest contribution to the analysis of argumentation was his observation that, at a minimum, all persuasive statements are backed by a warrant—that is, an underlying principle or general statement—with its own supportive facts, or backing, that supports the relation of the datum to the claim, and helps that relation to seem logical and well-reasoned, and the claim itself therefore to be convincing. Warrants, then, typically either implicitly or explicitly, justify the connections that speakers (or writers) work to make between empirical "facts" and their interpretation, and, by extension, their implications for action. The function of warrants as supports for empirically based claims makes Toulmin's model highly applicable in the present context.

Nearly 50 years after its original publication, Toulmin's work remains the best known and most frequently applied "grammar" of how communicatively competent individuals make arguments in real-life contexts. Its relative simplicity as well as its intuitive logic suggests that it has wide applicability across a broad range of contexts, from the analysis of newspaper editorials to legal arguments to academic research articles—indeed, to arguments made about almost any human social situation. Yet it is also not without significant operational drawbacks as an analytical tool. First, Toulmin's model was designed to explain the structure of individual arguments of the sort made directly and clearly by speakers, rather than the more complex, multiple arguments of an extended text, such as a research article. Second, Toulmin's model implies that arguments are made by speakers or writers in succinct utterances that can be lifted whole from a text and analytically dissected with relatively little, if any, interpretive license being taken. However, in actual texts, arguments are frequently not put forward in such direct and succinct fashion; instead, they are interwoven with other arguments in ways that make them difficult to separate, they may be implied rather than stated, or they may be discontinuous and extend across multiple parts of a text. Thus, while Toulmin's work does come closer to explaining the ways that arguments are made by people in everyday contexts than, for example Aristotelian syllogisms ("Where there are clouds, it will rain; there are clouds; therefore it will rain") do, it is still a step or two removed from fully capturing the complexity of the language and strategies people use when they speak or write in extended rhetorical contexts. This issue is somewhat mitigated, however, in the context of the following analyses, which focus on how a single element within an article, social theory, functions across each article generally as well as within individual points, or claims, made by the authors.

### Example one: social theory as foundational premise

The first example of social theory's use within published research is a study of how children use software intended to both entertain and educate them within an after school program, "Engineering Play: Children's Software and the Cultural Politics of Edutainment," by Mizuko Ito, published in the Australian journal, *Discourse*, in 2006. The article begins with a short history of three genres of educational software, entertainment (with little or no school-based content), authoring (not described), and the genre the article focuses on, edutainment (software designed to both entertain and educate). It continues with a review of the history of educational toys, which are described as a preoccupation of middle-class parents since the early nineteenth century, and of the desire to ameliorate a more general tension between work and recreation that is characteristic of industrialized societies. Ito then characterizes the history of software design for children in analogous terms, tracing its history from the early 1980s, when designers strove to design programs that infused academic content within challenging problem-solving programs, to more recent attempts, in the wake of increased emphasis on high-stakes testing and industry mergers, to design software that is more formulaic in design (and therefore cheaper to make) and more focused on the development of expertise within the game and habits of winning (at all costs) than on the acquisition of content-based knowledge.

In the second half of the article, Ito presents data from a study of how children participating in an after-school program in California called the 5th Dimension (5thD) used educational software, and in particular one of the later software programs, *The Island of Dr. Brain*, a problem-solving game in which players progress to higher levels of difficulty after solving problems that bring them points or symbolic rewards, such as magic tokens, whose accumulation leads to even greater symbolic rewards. As Ito notes, "*The Island of Dr. Brain* is part of this cultural construction and display of a form of competition that is institutionally separate from schooling but is tied to a related discourse and habitus of achievement" (Ito 2006: 50). Tensions were produced within the 5thD program between participating children, who focused on winning, and the participating undergraduate volunteers from local universities who prioritized the learning of content, and who continually noted that the children often found ways to circumvent learning by getting answers from peers in order to solve problems and move up in level of expertise. She highlights this analysis through the case of Roger, a child whose mastery and expertise at playing, but largely ignoring the academic content of the game, brought him great self-satisfaction and status among the other children in the program.

The presentation of data from the 5thD program and the case of Roger provides evidence in support of Ito's argument about the capitalist trajectory and ideology of the children's software industry. In conclusion, Ito writes, "Early edutainment developers hoped to put accessible technical tools in the hands of the disenfranchised, alleviating the oppressiveness of dominant notions of education." The realization of that promise, however, has been lost at least temporarily: "Contexts of play and informal learning, while seemingly marginal to the high stakes contestations over educational sorting and achievement, are sites that demonstrate the alignments and disjunctures between the cultural and social structures of children's lives." There is a need, she concludes, "to imagine alternative genres of participation that are both compelling and (economically and culturally) sustainable" (Ito 2006: 158).

"Engineering Play" provides an interesting illustration of Toulmin's concept of warrants as assumptions that support the linking of data to claims. In this case, an historical narrative stretching back to the early nineteenth century (the beginning of the Industrial Revolution), grounded in a neo-Marxist critique of the ideological effects of capitalism supports, or frames, an analysis of findings from an after-school program that leads to the claim that the academic value of children's software programs is being compromised in favor of capitalist values, namely winning and getting ahead at all costs. Social theory in the form of a discourse about relations among education, economics, and culture with striking resemblance to the writing of a broad range of theorists including Bourdieu, Gramsci, Freire, and Althusser among others is detectable in nearly every paragraph of the article; indeed, it is the foundation on which the article's analysis and conclusions rest. Yet, in only two instances—a brief reference to Vygotsky's (1978) Zone of Proximal Development on page 151 and a direct reference to Althusser's (1971) concept of interpellation, or the hailing of Roger as an expert on page 157—is any theory ever explicitly referenced, even though terms such as *habitus* on p. 50 (Bourdieu 1990) and more general phrases like "sites of production and consumption" on p. 158 are routinely used throughout the article.

In addition, social theory's absent presence as a warrant linking data and claims is accompanied by a number of other related warrants within the article, such as the assumption that children's software designers have a responsibility to produce and market programs in which educational content is more inescapable, and the assumption that "we" (the readers and the author) see the world in the same way and understand how evil the logic of capitalist practice is. Applying Toulmin's model also reveals the lack of backing, or evidence in support of the article's warranting assumptions, as well as a lack of qualification of the author's claims or rebuttal to any qualifications.

### Example two: social theory as focusing lens

A second, more explicit and complex use of social theory as a warrant is found in "Who Fired First? Students' Construction of Meaning from One Textbook Account of the Israeli-Arab Conflict," by Dan A. Porat, and published in the Canadian journal, *Curriculum Inquiry*, in 2006. Porat's article begins by noting an explicit set of changes in Israeli history textbooks in 1999, away from portrayals of Israelis as the consistent victims of Arab aggression, and toward a more ambivalent account of Israeli–Arab relations, changes that marked "a quiet revolution" (p. 251) in the teaching of history in Israel. But Porat points out that reading is often not a practice in which intended meanings are consumed whole by readers. The changes would be revolutionary only "if in fact the students internalize the textbook account as it appears on the page" (p. 252).

Porat cites Bakhtin's (1973) notion of *hidden dialogicality* to argue that Israelis read the new accounts in dialogue with what they have previously read and learned about the history of Israeli–Arab conflict. The body of the article illustrates this point by describing three theoretically grounded ways that students and parents in Israel interpreted an ambivalent account of an incident that occurred in 1920 at the settlement of Tel Hai, in which Israeli settlers and Arabs clashed, and a Zionist leader, Joseph Trumpeldor, was killed. In previous textbook accounts, Trumpeldor was portrayed as a valiant hero, who stood up against Arab aggression and paid the ultimate price. The more recent account, however, described the incident as having little significance in itself. It left the issue of who fired the first shot unanswered, and instead invited readers to reflect on the symbolic meaning that it had been given over time rather than as an event in itself.

Porat draws from interpretations given to the recent account by students and a parent at a left-wing Israel secondary school and students at a right-wing Talmudic school in Israel. True to his introductory Bakhtinian frame, the two sides have very different readings, which reflect their own political orientations. Porat's purpose is to use the differences to illustrate three different reading processes, which are warranted by three different theories of reading. Borrowing from Jauss (1982), who in turn borrows from the hermeneutics of Gadamer (1994), he shows how Jacob, the Israeli parent of a child at the left-wing school fuses his *horizon of expectations* about the textbook as a genre (that it will interpret history in a patriotic, skewed way that distorts unpleasant facts) with the horizon of the text itself, to conclude that it must have been the Jews who fired first, since that is what the ambiguity of the text on this point is probably trying to cover up. Porat then draws on the work of literary theorist Wolfgang Iser (1979), to show how the ambiguity of the first shot serves as a *gap in the text* that is filled in one way by Michael, a student at the right-wing Talmudic school, who concludes it was the Arabs who fired first, and by Natalie, the daughter of Jacob, who fills in the same gap by concluding that the Jews fired first. Third, he draws on the neo-Vygotskian work of James Wertsch (2002), to explain how Nathan, a student at the left-wing school, integrated the fictionalized narrative of a recent movie version of the Tel Hai incident, in which a mentally disturbed Israeli woman grabs a gun and fires wildly, triggering responses from both Israelis and Arabs, as a source of causality that the ambiguous textbook account did not supply.

As in Example One, social theory in "Who Fired First?" functions as a warrant that supports the linking of empirical evidence (the readings of three students and a parent) to a claim about the interpretability of historical texts, but with some significant differences. First, Porat's use of social theory is far more explicit than Ito's; he cites particular theorists and applies their ideas directly to his interpretation of the students' readings. He also cites previous empirical research studies as backing for the general warrant of the study's opening claim that we make sense of texts in light of what we already know about them and their content. Second, his use of theory has more of an *ad hoc* quality to it than does Ito's, who does cite the work of Vygotsky and Althusser to make specific points, but whose broader social theoretical framework remains consistent, if implicit, throughout the article. In Toulminian terms, Porat qualifies and rebuts his argument by acknowledging this *ad hoc* quality in his use of "conflicting theoretical viewpoints; yet I believe that in interpreting the real world we cannot limit ourselves to an orthodox viewpoint propounded by one 'truthful' theory. Rather, we should apply different theories, even conflicting ones, wherever they assist us best in interpreting the data" (p. 256).

### Example three: social theory as narrative scaffold

A third and even more complex example of the use of social theory is "'They Won't Let Us Play ... Unless You're Going out with One of Them': Girls, Boys, and Butler's 'Heterosexual Matrix' in the Primary Years," by Emma Renold, which appeared in the *British Journal of Sociology of Education* in 2006. The article opens with an extended review of research and theory on the topic of gender and sexuality in the primary (ages 4–11) school years. Renold argues that although childhood sexuality, particularly for girls, is often considered a taboo subject, there is significant evidence available that it also preoccupies many parents, educators, and children. She frames her discussion of the dynamics of childhood sexuality with a discussion of Judith Butler's (1990, 1993) concept of the "hegemonic heterosexual matrix," a discursive formation by which "children's normative gender identities are inextricably embedded and produced within hegemonic (normative and dominant) representations of heterosexuality" (Renold 2006: 491). Renold's discussion of the dynamics of this matrix is backed by extensive citations and descriptions of previous research, including not only discussions of the performance of normative heterosexuality by children, but also the performative "queering," or challenging of heterosexual hegemony, during moments when high-status boys recognized for their masculinity by their peers "act gay" or through "tomboy" behavior by girls.

Renold's use of social theory throughout the article is so ubiquitous and well-developed that at times her data seem to take a subordinate, supporting role within the article's main arguments, and to scaffold, rather than simply warrant, her ethnographic narrative. Renold seems to intend this reading herself, when she notes, "I will be revisiting data that enable an analysis of how Butler's ubiquitous heterosexual matrix operates to regulate boy-girl intimacies, from physical proximity to hetero-relationship cultures within the subject positions 'girlfriend' and 'boyfriend' in a range of expected and unexpected ways" (p. 492)—in other words, using data to illustrate a pre-existing theoretical position. She does not merely smatter her discussion with anecdotal evidence, however, but instead presents extended portraits of particular children from a larger ethnographic study as illustrations, first, of normative heterosexual performances, and then of the ways in which both girls and boys find ways to challenge, if only temporarily, normative behavior and to have relationships with each other that are not completely sexualized in their orientation. Her presentation and discussion of these "queer" moments from her data provide evidence in support of her concluding argument, in which she cites the "need to problematize adult-centric tendencies to conceptualize young children's preoccupation with boyfriends and girlfriends solely as practicing and performing 'older' (hetero)genders/sexualities" (p. 505).

Rhetorically, "They Won't Let Us Play" represents the most extensive departure from the standard "let the data speak for themselves" approach typical of traditional social science and educational research of the three examples thus far. Theory is placed in the foreground of Renold's argument, and data is used to illustrate, not generate, theory. It is aligned with Butler's theory and provides a living portrait of the hegemonic complexities of a ubiquitous heterosexual matrix. Yet a close reading of the article does not leave the sense that Renold "found what she was looking for" in her research, or that her analysis is lacking at all in rigor or is otherwise suspected or misguided. The article's veracity is due, in part, I suspect, to the quality of her data and the care with which portions were selected for inclusion. Reading the transcribed remarks of the children's interactions with each other and adult interviewers brought a level of verisimilitude to the discussion that would have been lacking otherwise. But the article's credibility is also attributable, from a Toulminian perspective, to the extensive backing for her theoretical warrant that Renold provides in the form of previous research, and to the qualifications, or questions, she raises in her conclusion about whether the gendered and sexual performances of children should be interpreted as preparations for adulthood, or as performances with more immediate outcomes.

### Example four: social theory as dialectical scaffold

An article that similarly foregrounds theoretical discourse, but for the purpose of challenging or revising some of its concepts through the presentation of findings that are in some ways at odds with theory is "Newly Betwixt and Between: Revising Liminality in the Context of a Teacher

Preparation Program," by Alison Cook-Sather and published in the United States by *Anthropology and Education Quarterly* in 2006. The article begins with a lengthy discussion of Victor Turner's (1974, 1981) description of ritual initiation processes within cultural groups. In Turner's account, which was based on anthropological studies of rites of passage within African cultures in the 1950s and 1960s, initiates pass from one stage of life to another, such as from childhood into adulthood, from single life into marriage, or from the position of layperson to priest, by passing through a liminal, threshold stage of becoming, in which, as neither their former nor their future self, they are for a short time and space able to contemplate (and critique) their roles and the meaning of the world from a position that is free of sanction.

Cook-Sather describes the short and intense period of formal teacher preparation within US colleges and universities as one such liminal period of formation. Her innovation is to argue that the use of e-mail exchanges in her program between mentor teachers and students offers a quality of liminality that is different from the condition of liminality Turner described, but one that is uniquely suited to postmodernity:

> Within rites of passage such as teacher preparation, rather than groups of neophytes moving from one kind of collective state into a new collective state, we must reckon with and nurture a more complex, individual, and contextual sense of self developed through a more complex, multiply informed process of identify formation. (p. 121)

Whereas Turner saw initiates moving together through formal, uniform processes, Cook-Sather argues that the use of e-mail between students and mentors serves the purpose of helping students to develop individual selves that respond more directly to the unique situations they encounter in their separate field placements. The asynchronous quality of e-mail and the fact that it takes place in parallel with multiple other formative experiences also differentiates e-mail as a space with a liminal quality that is different from the ways in which Turner's theory has been typically applied, yet uniquely suited to the development of a professional self within the contemporary world.

Structurally and rhetorically, the article is organized as a dialogue between Turner's theory and Cook-Sather's data. The paper opens with an introductory discussion of Turner's concept of liminality and the ritual process, but moves in its second page to the introduction of Cook-Sather's teacher preparation program, followed by a section on Methods and Participants. From this point, the discussion alternates between more detailed discussions of particular aspects of Turner's theory followed by some alteration of that theory through its application to the data of the e-mail exchanges in Cook-Sather's program. Most of the external sources cited by Cook-Sather are from anthropological studies outside of education, although there are a few studies of the use of e-mail and the Internet in other contexts. From a Toulminian perspective, the differences that Cook-Sather notes between Turner's classic description of liminality and the liminality of the e-mail exchanges she studied, warranted by a discussion of Toulmin's original theory of ritual processes and Cook-Sather's own discussion of differences between the societies he studied and the world of her students, and backed by relatively few previous studies, leads her to claim that e-mail exchanges represent a modification in the definition of a liminal space and the ritual process of transformation that Turner proposed. Qualification and rebuttal of this claim per Toulmin's model is missing from Cook-Sather's argument. In summary, the article and its arguments provide an interesting example of a very different relationship between theory and data analysis than the previous three examples—an example in which the research itself reciprocally is built upon and builds theoretical knowledge.

### Cross-case comparison: uses of theory

In each of the preceding four examples, social theory plays a major role in framing the analysis of data, in making the point of view of the researcher explicit, and in the production of new knowledge and understandings of the phenomena under investigation. Without the use of theory, Ito's complaint about the failure of edutainment to educate might be understandable; but her placement of her analysis within a broader understanding of the history of educational toys and their cultural significance would not have been possible. Similarly, without recourse to social theory, Porat may have been able to demonstrate the claim that readers' own prior knowledge can have a dramatic impact on the ways they read a text, but his description of three different processes whereby this occurs depended almost entirely on previous theoretical work. Renolds may have been able to document the ways that children talk about their gendered and sexualized relations with each other, but without the support of Butler's work she would have lacked the language to characterize the normative and queering forces that structured the students' performances as normative or queer. Finally, without Turner's theory of ritual processes and his description of liminality, Cook-Sather's work would have lacked a foil, and would have been little more than an interesting account of how students in a teacher preparation program used e-mail to discuss ideas with their mentors.

The application of Toulmin's model of argument, however, foregrounds very different uses and effects of social theory in each example. Ito makes reference to social theory throughout her analysis, but the references are largely implicit and without backing or qualification. Porat is more explicit in his use of social theory, but his use has an *ad hoc*, almost opportunistic quality. Renold makes explicit use of Butler's work and backs her theoretical warrants with extensive reference to and discussion of previous research; she also uses theory and the analysis of her own data to raise additional questions and challenges to the field of gender studies in the conclusion of her study. And Cook-Sather uses data from e-mail exchanges to challenge and extend the meaning of Turner's concept of liminality within (postmodern) ritual processes.

These four examples also provide a graphic illustration of the first axiom of this book that data are always interpreted and that they never speak for themselves, and in addition, that the more open researchers are in explicating the warrants they use for their interpretations, or claims, the more rhetorically open—and convincing—their arguments are likely to be. However, the differences among them in the ways and purposes for which theory was used may also, in turn, raise questions about whether there is a "right" way or a "better" or "worse" way to use social theory within social science and educational research.

Responding to that question brings us back to the second axiom of the book, about the inherently rhetorical nature of research as an activity. Answering the question of what is a better or worse use of social theory may depend, at least in part, on whom one is writing for and what one's purposes are. For example, it may be that the lack of direct citation and referencing of social theory in Ito's article was due to an assumed prior knowledge on the part of readers of *Discourse*, a journal with a strong, long-standing tradition grounded in neo-Marxist theory. Porat's *ad hoc* use of social theories of reading may be explainable, at least in part, to his own research background and specialization as a history educator, rather than as someone with interests in reading comprehension research or literary theory. In other words, his interests and purposes in writing were not to develop a theory of how students read textbooks, but only to make the argument that changing the language of history textbooks may be unlikely to change the culturally charged meanings that students and their parents give to them.

The effectiveness of more extensive uses of social theory, as in the examples of the articles by Renold and Cook-Sather, may also be evaluated in this way. Renold's extensive and complex use of Butler's work, combined with her citation of previous research in the field of gender studies and the challenge to refine understandings of how children's sexuality is understood in terms of their childhood rather than future adult lives, suggests that she is writing to an audience composed of two concentric circles: a small core group of feminist poststructuralist educational researchers, and a larger group of academics with an interest in the sociology of gender and sexuality. Cook-Sather, on the other hand, seems to be writing for a broader audience of researchers in teacher education interested in an anthropological/sociological view of the process of teacher preparation, rather than for a core of anthropologists with a strong interest in rituality and Turner's work.

Which approach is "better" or "best," then? From a Habermasian perspective, I would argue that arguments that make their reasoning processes more transparent, that are more detailed in their explication of their warrants and the backing that supports them, and that take care not merely to accept social theories as given but that engage in some critical comparison of findings and their fit with theories, are more likely to be accepted by a wider range of readers as valid. In the present examples, I would argue that although Ito and Porat's work raises interesting and important issues within their respective fields, the lack of citations and backing within "Engineering Play" and the lost opportunity in "Who Fired First?" to work toward a synthesis of the theories used limits the validity of their arguments and their applicability in other contexts. By contrast, the extended theoretical discussion and backing of "They Won't Let Us Play" and the tension between findings and theory in "Newly Betwixt and Between" increases both the validity and the potential of these studies to add to general bodies of knowledge about children's sexualities and ritual processes within postindustrial societies.

Finally, the use of social theory within these last two examples also suggests another use of social theory within educational research, and one that may help qualitative and ethnographic researchers formulate a response to the charge that data collected within a single locale cannot yield findings with general significance. In both examples, although data were only collected in a few locales, the act of relating findings to more general theories of sexuality and ritual processes amplified the meanings that could be taken from them in significant ways. This is not to say that Renold's or Cook-Sather's conclusions are in any way "the last word" on the issues they raise, or that data collected in other locations and analyzed using the same theoretical frameworks might not revise or extend their conclusions, but that the extensiveness and openness of their reasoning processes gives them a credibility and validity that must be taken into account in future qualitative *and* experimentally based studies. Their findings, in sum, add to what is known about their respective topics in ways that cannot be denied, and in ways that suggest possibilities for using social theories as frameworks for the construction of general bodies of educational knowledge. This is a possibility that I am only raising in this chapter but will develop in greater detail in Chapter Five.

## Summary and conclusion

In this chapter, the example of phonemic/phonological research provided the context for an extended discussion of the implications of two axioms that are central to the arguments of this book: (1) that *data never speak for themselves*; and (2) that *research is a rhetorical activity*. A discussion of the tensions that the failure to adequately address these axioms has produced within educational research led to a proposal for a different approach within educational studies. That approach rejects attempts to deny or compensate for these axioms' consequences, as though they were problems to be solved, and instead urges that researchers begin to think more openly about how they make arguments and to acknowledge and make explicit the assumptions, or theories, that warrant their interpretations of data. In the second half of the chapter, I presented an analysis of four recently published educational research articles using Toulmin's model of argumentation, as a way of demonstrating a range of possible ways that social theory might be used in the production of knowledge about educational phenomena that was both valid and, as my final comments suggest, that could contribute to the development of bodies of general knowledge within education.

However, while this discussion and the four examples may provide a portrait of social theory's potential in the making of arguments, they are analyses conducted after the fact of the research itself and so are likely to provide little practical instruction about the process of using theory within an ongoing research context. In the next two chapters I turn to these more practical issues, framed in a fictional narrative of one research project and with the intent of providing a concrete example of social theory's possible roles throughout a research project, from its conception to its design and data collection to its analytical, interpretive, and publication stages.

# Chapter 3

# Framing research theoretically

## Introduction

This chapter and the next turn to more practical matters with regard to the uses of social theory in educational research. Chapter Three describes possible uses of social theory as a resource in the making of good arguments, beginning with the conceptualization of a study and continuing through its design and data collection. Chapter Four begins with formal analysis of the data and continues the description of theories' use through the stages of formal argumentation, or writing and publication.

In order to illustrate the uses of social theory across the research process in the most concrete, practical terms possible, these two chapters will alternate passages of exposition with a narrative, fictional composite of a novice researcher who decides to study an instructional unit in one of his classes. Although Rick Chavez, his teaching situation, and his students are not "real" in the sense that they have existed as actual individuals, as representations of attitudes, practices, curriculum, and social and cultural conditions found in the secondary schools and environs of major cities across the postindustrial world, they are very real indeed. They exist as portraits drawn from the experiences of many teachers and students in both my own teaching and research and that of my former graduate advisees; indeed, all of the events described are adaptations of situations that either they or I have experienced. Combining the experiences of multiple individuals and actual events provides a level of both illustrative complexity and verisimilitude that would not have been possible had I drawn from a single historical instance.

Rick Chavez teaches modern history and current events to mid-level secondary students (ages 15–17) in a publicly funded school on the edge of a major city. His students are a diverse group, both culturally and economically. The community in which he teaches is a residential area that was built in the early part of the twentieth century as a middle- to upper-middle-class suburb of the city. By the end of the same century, this neighborhood was eclipsed by newer communities farther outside the city center, and today is home to a population of largely middle- to working-class families. It is a relatively stable community: Most of Rick's students have lived nearly their entire lives there, and the rest are from families that have immigrated in the past 20 years. Most of Rick's students are from two-parent households, although a significant number are also from single-parent homes. Nearly all the parents work full-time, and are employed as shop owners, office workers, and in public service professions such as nursing or teaching.

Culturally, approximately two-thirds of Rick's students are from families who have lived in this country for more than a century; about half of these are of color and half are White. The other third are from first- or second-generation families from a very diverse group of Asian Pacific, Central Asian and Islamic, African, and Caribbean and Latin American countries. Most of these students speak English as a first language, with varying degrees of proficiency in their parents' first languages. Rick identifies strongly with the backgrounds of this latter third. His parents emigrated from Central America during the turmoil of the early 1980s when he was an infant. Rick grew up in the city and has never returned to the country of his birth. His early years were spent in a Spanish-language neighborhood in the city, but when he was nine the family moved to an English-speaking community next to the one in which he now teaches, and he lost some of his fluency in Spanish, although he retains close cultural ties to the Latino community. He has invested in a satellite dish, and regularly watches football matches on Spanish-language channels from Mexico, Argentina, and other Latin American countries. Rick was a good student and particularly enjoyed secondary school. His parents wanted him to study law, but a stint as a volunteer in a school and a later internship in a law firm during his university years convinced him that he'd much rather be a teacher.

Rick is 28 years old and recently married to Gwen, who teaches Spanish at another nearby secondary school; they have no children, but hope to start a family soon. He has been teaching for five years and is at a point in his career where he is beginning to question his long-term commitment to the profession. His first few years were spent developing a repertoire of managerial and pedagogical skills that fit his temperament and that of his students and school.

There were also rocky moments for him in terms of his own racial identity and that of his students. Rick entered his classroom one morning to find the word *spic* written on his blackboard. On another occasion, he returned to his classroom after lunch to find a handful of "Mexican jumping beans" and a note labeling them on his desk. The anonymity of these hateful experiences made him "a little paranoid," he told Gwen, but he also resolved not to give in to these feelings or show resentment toward his students. By the end of the year, there were no more incidents. Rick sensed that he had won the students' confidence and respect the day that blond-haired, blue-eyed Maria mentioned to him after class that she "had a Spanish name, too, just like (him)." *Spanish!*—Rick thought afterward; was that how they were now rationalizing his ethnicity? Was he now "Spanish," and therefore "European," and not a "spic" anymore to them?!

This experience left Rick with a sense of alienation from and edginess about his students that he continued to struggle with afterwards. In an effort to put these incidents behind him, Rick tried to "compartmentalize" his life, living as a Latino in his personal life and assuming the more "secular" practices of a (White) middle-class professional at school. In his second year of teaching he threw himself into the pedagogical and curricular aspects of his work. He joined his national professional organization and adopted its discourse of best practice as his own. He tried some of the ideas from its journal and even attended one of its annual conferences. Through a deliberate process of self-conscious reflection on the outcomes of his different activities, he gradually developed a routine that kept students largely on-task and that seemed to produce good results for most of them. Around the end of his third year, he caught himself thinking one day that teaching was "like breathing" to him, it seemed so natural and almost reflexive as a process.

But recently, doubt and dissatisfaction with what and how he is teaching have begun to nag at Rick. During a presentation on the Second World War one day, he looked up to see three students asleep in the back rows of his class. Rick dutifully walked back to the students to rouse them, and on the way he noticed multiple notes, cell phones, and even several hand-held electronic games in his students' hands, concealed beneath their textbooks. Later, in a conversation with Gwen, he lamented that sometime in the last four years he had become "the most boring teacher on earth." "Or is it the material?" she asked. Placing himself in his students' perspective, Rick suddenly realized that for more than half of the class his presentation from an

Anglo perspective of the War and its consequences must seem alien, if not alienating.

A few days later, Rick had his students take out a sheet of paper and write on it everything that came to mind when they heard the phrase, "The Second World War."

"That'll be short work," quipped one student, Tom.

"Just write whatever comes to mind," Rick reassured them. He began to walk among the desks, joking with students and patiently, quietly urging them to write.

"How much do you want?" asked a girl, Angelina.

"Are you marking this?" Sanjay wanted to know.

The students' papers were, Rick thought, remarkably empty. A few thought their grandfathers may have been in the War; some knew about Hitler and drew swastikas in the margins of their papers; others wrote a few sentences about the Japanese and Hiroshima. The next day he asked his class directly why they had written so little. Hadn't they studied this in a lower level? Hadn't they seen movies, or watched programs on TV? "We never got that far," Angelina said. Another student admitted he hadn't paid attention and "didn't watch that stuff." In a staff meeting later in the afternoon, several teachers were complaining about their students' lack of motivation and interest in school. Rick spoke up, told his story, and then suggested, "We need to think about this in a different way. I don't know, maybe more anthropologically."

"*Anthropologically!*" Rita, a teacher with 23 years' experience, laughed. "Where'd you learn a word like that—in your grad-u-ate class?!"

## First encounters with social theory

Research that opens itself to social theory typically begins not with an academic question but more personally, with a sense of dissonance between what is expected or looked for and what has been experienced. In most everyday narratives of secondary schooling, formal education figures as the ladder to upward social mobility. Teachers have knowledge and students come to school to get it, so that they can progress to higher levels that accord greater status and the opportunity, finally, to acquire the professional knowledge of a doctor or a lawyer or an accountant or business manager. There is an occasional acknowledgment that much of the academic content of schooling is "dry," or distant from students' lived experience, but because students "will need it later on," it must be taught and students must learn it anyway. And so when students balk at an assignment or appear disinterested or claim they do not know what they should have already learned, there can only be a few possible explanations. Either there has been a moral failure on the part of students' communities and families to value education, or the students are distracted by developmental issues (they are "hormones with feet," as I once heard a teacher describe her 14–15-year-old students), or perhaps the teacher has not done what she or he could to "make learning fun." Accounts like these typically lead to tactical, short-term responses designed to alleviate, and then only temporarily, the frustrations of a set of conditions that are characterized as not only endemic, but inevitable, as part of the "nature" of society and of adolescence and learning itself. These narrative explanations are so prevalent and so powerful that few teachers, myself included, have escaped from participating in them during their careers, and fewer still examine alternative, "anthropological" narratives of schooling with any seriousness.

Realizing that one needs a new way of seeing and understanding the world is an exciting moment, but it is also one fraught with challenges. The theoretical perspectives most readily available and accessible oftentimes do not fully challenge worldviews, but instead rework them in different terms. For example, many years ago, in search of a different way of thinking about the teaching of literature, I turned to the work of the psychologist Carl Jung (1968) and of Joseph Campbell (1968), a comparative mythologist who had recently appeared in a popular documentary series on public television in the USA. I had been teaching on the Navajo Indian Reservation in Arizona and was much taken by what I perceived to be close structural parallels between the Navajo creation story, with its figures of Spider Woman and the Hero Twins and its Twelve Holy People, and the Roman story of Romulus and Remus, and the Christian tradition of the Twelve Apostles. The significance of particular numbers and cycles—three, four, seven, twelve—across cultures seemed to me to conjure a single Great Myth that I believed would energize my teaching and my multicultural students in the urban school where I taught after leaving the Reservation. I made the acquaintance of another teacher in my school who was interested in Jung, and together we attended weekend lectures and discussed readings.

My students did respond to my new comparative teaching approach, and for a while I believed I was on to something revolutionary in literature education. But the more I read, the more forced the unity of Campbell's "monomyth" seemed. Campbell's figure of the individualistic male hero also seemed less and less universal and more and more American to me as I read, while both his and Jung's practices of subsuming the stories of other cultures within a structure that never strayed far from the contours of the narratives of the Christian West began to strike me as terribly colonialist, and my own attempts to adapt these principles in my teaching as culturally imperialist as well.

It was not until I returned to graduate school and began to read educational research that made use of broad social and cultural theories that I gained access to a body of literature and a way of reading and integrating theory, and analysis that challenged my own cultural norms and assumptions. This is also the approach I would advocate for others in finding a body of social theory that informs a particular situation, although I would also warn against accepting one researcher's approach to using a theorist or school of theory as authoritative, and against embracing any single perspective too fully, especially in the initial stages of inquiry. From the beginning, the use of social theory in educational research is a hermeneutic process, in the Gadamerian (Gadamer 1994) sense: One moves from the particulars of observed experience out to comparison and contrast with broader, theoretical accounts, and back to observed experience, over multiple cycles and, where and when possible, across different theoretical perspectives. All the while, other comparisons, among previous research studies and between those studies' uses of social theory and the original texts of social theorists and their commentators, also need to be made.

There is systematicity and rigor to this process, but it is not overly procedural, and although the cycles of comparison and contrast between and among observed experience and theory should become more focused over multiple repetitions, the process ends only when the inquiry itself is concluded. In this approach, the quality of one's inquiry is entirely dependent not on a lock-step method or set of steps per se, but rather on the degree of rigor and reflexivity, or skepticism and self-examination, of the relations between one's data and one's theory. Moreover, in relating observed experience to theory, the process is not unidirectional; social theory is not simply used to make sense of observed experience, one's experiences also give sense and understanding to social theory as well. The reciprocity of the sense-making process may also explain the frustration I have heard graduate students occasionally voice over the need to "get a theoretical frame" for their research, especially when they approach the search process without first having focused on a situation or set of experiences that they are interested in making theoretical sense of. Theories in general, and social theories in particular, are far more dependent on empirical experience to give them life and meaning than these students, or for that matter, many academics, would acknowledge.

Rick was taken off-guard by Rita's reaction to his remark, but not personally so. Although he was enrolled in a masters program at a local university, he had never taken a course in anthropology. Beyond the racial incidents that marked his first year of teaching, Rick did not conceive of education in overtly cultural terms. His comment in the staff meeting, made spontaneously and without much prior thought, was the first time he had openly articulated the idea that there were forces much broader than his teaching or his students' and their families' attitudes that were responsible for the lack of enthusiasm and engagement in his classroom. Before the staff meeting, Rick had participated multiple times in conversations in which the normative account of school failure had prevailed, but his off-hand comment and Rita's reaction to it prompted him to rethink these explanations.

For one thing, Rick knew that his students were smart. He was almost certain they knew exactly what they were doing, even if they didn't always know why they were doing it, and so it seemed unlikely to him that they would be "screwing themselves" in the ways that teachers typically assume they are when students opt out of participating in their own education. Maybe they understood, even if only subliminally, something that he did not about the educational process. Second, Rick had already realized that writing students off as the products of bad homes, or as racist, or hormonally drugged, or blaming himself or his subject for being boring were excuses that did not lead to productive responses to the issues he was facing. And finally, Rick knew that his problems were not tactical (he was popular with students; he was efficient and up-to-date methodologically; he seldom had a serious discipline problem in his classes anymore), but strategic. They had to do with issues outside his classroom that were permeating the milieu, or social atmosphere and practices of those within.

The courses that Rick was taking in his masters program had so far been general in nature (a course in the history and philosophy of education; another in teaching students with special needs) and had not addressed the lack of interest or motivation he had noticed in his classroom. He had, however, begun to wonder if there was a body of research in this area, and to imagine how it might frame the problem. He was hopeful that his current course, on the psychology and cognition of learning, might offer some insight. In this course, he read primary works and other applications of social constructivists (Vygotsky 1978; Wertsch 1985), situated cognition (Brown et al.

1989; Lave and Wenger 1991), and motivational theorists (Bandura 1986; Deci and Ryan 1985), and found these to be interesting ways of thinking about organizing school tasks. However, he had already organized his students into small groups and given them challenging group tasks in which completion was contingent on collaboration; and he'd worked hard to personalize topics in history, drawing on differences in his students' cultural backgrounds, using multimedia in his presentations and raising questions that challenged his students to see themselves and their families in historical context. His students responded, but he still sensed that much of the time they were just "going through the motions," and that in the end, their engagement was largely contingent on the mark they needed or hoped to receive.

When an elective graduate course was listed for the following semester titled "Secondary Schooling in Social Context," Rick enrolled. The course was a departure from others that he had taken in his program. It was structured as a series of seminars rather than lectures, the required readings for the course were ethnographic and sociological rather than psychological or philosophical in their orientation, and there was a final project for the course rather than a paper or an examination. Rick was intrigued by the readings for the course, even if he was put off by some of the politics, which were more strident and farther to the left than he would normally place himself, and some of the terminology, which struck him at first as needlessly elaborated in its endless definition and redefinition of common words such as *production, reproduction,* and *agency.* But gradually, he began to connect the portraits of adolescent resistance and negotiation in studies such as those by Willis (1977), Weis (1990), Foley (1990), McLaren (1986), and McRobbie (1991) to the behavior—the *practices,* if you will—of his own students, and to see them and himself as actors in a much larger political, economic, and historical drama that extended into and well beyond his own classroom over the course of a single year.

## Student resistance: production and/or reproduction?

Since the 1970s, the social theoretical literature on secondary schooling has provided one of the liveliest and longest-standing dialogues between theory and empirical evidence in all of educational research. To a far greater degree than infant or primary schools, where issues of cognitive and emotional development have typically been the focus of research, studies of secondary education have more frequently been framed in terms of schooling's economic imperatives, not only for individual students but for societies as well. As far back as the early 1960s, books such as *Education and the Cult of Efficiency* (Callahan 1962) noted the similarity in practices and organization between secondary schools and the workplace. In the 1970s, researchers took up a more overtly structuralist and highly determined view of secondary schooling. True to their Marxist roots, books such as *Schooling in Capitalist America* (Bowles and Gintis 1976) and *Reproduction in Education, Society, and Culture* (Bourdieu and Passeron 1977) argued that the purpose of schooling was to "reproduce the means of production"—that is, to ensure a differentiated supply of workers and managers who thought and acted like workers and managers and whose expectations and aspirations were also attuned to the needs of capitalism. In these studies, human agency, or the capacity of people to think and act for themselves rather than in over-determined response to their environment, was denied or largely ignored.

The question of exactly how schools condition students to assume the future identities and habits of one social class or another was not examined until the publication in 1977 (and in the USA in 1981) of *Learning to Labour: How Working Class Lads Get Working Class Jobs*, by Paul Willis, a British ethnographer at the Birmingham Centre for Contemporary Cultural Studies. Willis's study was revolutionary in its time, and remains to this day the book against which most other studies of student resistance and secondary education are conducted and written. Rather than describe social reproduction in education based on broad statistical and historical evidence as Callahan (1962) and Bourdieu and Passeron (1977) did, Willis presented a very detailed study of the attitudes and interactions with teachers, girlfriends, and peers of a group of working-class males in a secondary school in the English Midlands. He contrasted two groups of boys in the school: "ear'oles," boys who were compliant and cooperative, and whose career paths led to gray-collar (clerical and lower managerial) positions in the civil service and business, and the "lads," boys who largely resisted ideological messages about relations between school achievement and career advancement, by "having a laff," or acting out in class and in the hallways. He also noted similarities in form and effect between the lads' having a laff and their fathers' resistant behavior on the factory shop floor, and between the ways that the lads related to teachers and administrators, and their fathers' relations with shop foremen and managers. Willis championed the capacity of the lads to "partially penetrate" the ideology of schooling, that is, to see that their futures were likely no more and no less "bright" than those of the earnest, hard-working ear'oles, even as he noted that their resistance also seemed to socialize them to a life of manual labor. Rather than leave school as well-disciplined and compliant laborers, Willis's lads left with a strong, positive sense of being able to think for themselves and talk back to their future employers in ways that would ensure a degree of autonomy and self-determination about how (and how hard) they would labor.

Willis's study remains current today because of its portrayal of the lads' partial consciousness of their economic situation and assertion of agency, or the capacity to think and act for themselves, against the structures of the school and society at large. Later ethnographers of education (e.g. Dressman 1997; Foley 1990; Levinson *et al.*1996) built on the evidence that people are not helpless against the forces of society, but in fact are often highly creative and resourceful in finding ways to resist, evade, or take ironic advantage of the forces that would keep them in their economic, cultural, gendered, and/or sexual places. They also advanced the argument that over the long term, resistant actions can have a productive if not restructuring effect on the social and cultural order. Still other ethnographers and social theorists have responded to Willis's work in more critical terms, noting that however liberatory the lads' behavior might have been for themselves, it also carried with it strong elements of racism and sexism that were reproductive of White male dominance (e.g. McRobbie 1991; Dolby and Dimitriadis 2004).

The more studies of secondary schooling Rick read, the more he found himself making sense of his own teaching experiences through the *tropics*, or metaphoricity, of social and cultural production and reproduction. In the teachers' workroom one day he overheard the school social worker discussing with a group of teachers a visit she'd made to the home of Deidre, a girl in his third period history class who was expecting a baby toward the end of the school year. "Oh, yes, she'll be keeping it," the social worker remarked, "and she'll need home assignments to finish out the year." One of the teachers asked what reaction Deidre's family was having to the pregnancy. "Her mother's fine with it," the social worker reported. "And Deidre is also quite excited." She would not be marrying the father. "He's got visiting rights, and she'll have public assistance and stay at home with her mum, so everyone's happy," she noted. One teacher expressed annoyance, even shock, with "the irresponsibility of it all" and "the life that child is likely to have." Afterward, Rick realized that he was not as shocked or irritated by this news as the other teachers were or he would have been a year before, especially after he learned that Deidre's mother had been a teenager herself when Deidre was born. Instead, he saw Deidre, who did, in fact, seem to have a new glow of contentment about her, and whose attentiveness and written work had actually improved since the pregnancy, as realizing an important personal and cultural goal in her life, even if (or perhaps, slyly, because) it was "on the public dole"; he even caught himself grinning one day at the ironic and immediate way in which her condition leant new meaning to the terms *production* and *reproduction*.

In another case, after Darren, a boy in the same class as Deidre, refused to participate in class activities and was disruptive over two weeks, Rick asked for a conference with his father and the school's dean of students. In the meeting, the father explained apologetically to Rick, "I'm afraid I might be the cause of Darren's problems. You see, I've got my own roofing business and the money is good right now, so I told Darren that when he turned the legal age in a few weeks, he could leave school and join me." Rick was surprised at the father's directness, and did not know how to respond; but the dean apparently did. He pulled out Darren's files and suggested they go over his marks. "A C in mathematics," he noted. "And let's see, a D in English, and what's this—an F in physical education," he said, looking up.

The father turned to Darren in surprise. "An *F* in physical education? You're *failing* physical education?!"

"The comment from the teacher is that Darren isn't dressing and won't participate," the dean read.

The father was outraged. "I won't have it! You want to climb on roofs with me and sweat in the sun all day but you won't act like a man at school?!" He turned to Rick and the dean. "I'm sorry, Mr. Chavez. Darren won't be leaving school for now, at least until he brings all his grades up, especially in physical education. And he won't be causing you no more trouble in your class, either. Come on, boy." Rick was left to marvel after this incident at the power that an apparent blow to a father's sense of masculine identity might have on his son's education, and at the dean's reflexive understanding of the situation.

Rick's greatest insights, however, came as he began to revisit the dynamics of his interactions with students in his classes. One Friday, for example, toward the end of class Rick signaled a transition to review for a test he hoped to give on Monday. Just as he turned to distribute a review sheet, Luis, who knew from previous conversations about Rick's penchant for Latin American football, asked off-hand whom Rick favored in an upcoming match between a visiting team from Mexico City and the city's home team. Sensing a diversion, Rick reached for the pile of sheets and quickly said he thought Mexico City had the better goalee. "But what about Tyson (a home team star)?" asked Aakash. "And I hear that Sanchez (the goalee) has a pulled muscle and might not play." Against his better judgment, Rick turned and replied. Another student chimed in, then another, and then someone asked Rick if he'd ever played and what he remembered of games in Central America when he was a child, and he was off.

Just as Rick remembered that he was about to review for the test on Monday, he looked at the clock and saw that two minutes were left in the period. "Now, you guys," he smiled, "we have a test on Monday, and I've got these review sheets—"

"But what about the game?" asked Shawntay, whom Rick was sure had no interest in football at all. "You never told us who you really thought will win."

"Yes, I did," said Rick quickly, as he began to distribute the review sheets. But it was all over. The bell rang, and the students, smiling and laughing, quickly rose. "Now, WAIT a minute," Rick said. "Wait!" But the students were already up and out the door. *Wow*, Rick thought. He'd been caught in a "making out game" (Foley 1990). His students had played him perfectly to avoid having to study for the test over the weekend. And he—hadn't he been more than a little complicit in the ruse himself? What a little piece of theatre they'd pulled off, with him in a supporting role. Rick noted his own semi-conscious acquiescence to the students' ploy, and wondered to what extent his students had been aware of what they were doing. At the time, the interactions seemed so off-the-cuff and completely unplanned; in hindsight, so patterned and orchestrated.

Repeated incidents such as these confirmed for Rick that there was an underlying structure, or pattern of social and cultural practice in his and his students' interactions in school, that could not be denied or explained away in terms of random differences in personality or life history. At the same time, however, he also began to wonder whether the term *resistance* was a completely accurate descriptor of the multiple ways that he saw his students relating to his teaching and to school in general, or whether the processes of production/reproduction in much of the theory and research he was reading were as inevitable or relatively straightforward as they seemed.

For example, a number of his students, many of whom were first-generation immigrants, seemed quite diligent about their studies, even if they were not totally engaged. These were students who rarely participated willingly when he tried to conduct a discussion, but who turned in all their work and did well on tests and exams. Were these the ear'oles Willis described? Many of these students from previous years were now at university and, from what he had heard, were doing quite well in their studies. The sister of one of the students in this group was in medical school and hoped to become a cancer researcher when she graduated. These career paths did not seem socially reproductive at all, as Willis had described the fates of ear'oles. Rather, from almost any point of view, these students seemed to be very successful, even though, again, Rick wondered at how little creativity or engagement in his classes they showed, or how little they seemed to care personally about the issues he tried to raise in his instruction.

Then, one day, it struck him: *He'd* been one of these students when he was in secondary school; *he'd* been largely disengaged, too, at least until he reached university and got involved in some groups protesting US involvement in Latin America, and then he'd started to think about how important history was, and how little he really understood of who he was and how he'd gotten to be where he was. If not in secondary school, then at university he was a firebrand, all right, or at least he was no *ear'ole*—far from it. He *could* have been a lawyer, instead of a civil servant, teaching kids who didn't seem to care about what he had to share. The word *ear'ole* burned him the more he thought about it, as did the lack of any significant role for teaching or for curriculum, in the scenarios spun out by social theorists and ethnographies of schooling. These discourses suggested that the content and purpose of schooling *was* identity production and reproduction, rather than the acquisition of knowledge about history, literature, mathematics, the sciences, and so on. And, they seemed to be intent on reproducing *him* as a creature of the system, caught in the delusion that he was making a difference in his students' lives and in the world when in fact his teaching was little more than a distraction to his students and a cog in the machinery of the political and cultural economy.

## Connecting theory with research

To a greater extent than other areas of social theory, theories of social and cultural production and reproduction in secondary schooling have a long tradition of opening themselves to critique and revision. Willis's (1977) study and the work of structuralist and neo-Marxist theorists, such as Bourdieu and Passeron (1977) and Bowles and Gintis (1976) are regarded as the texts that each new study references, but the referencing is seldom completely reverent. Instead, each new ethnography, from Everhart (1983) to MacLeod (1987) to McRobbie (1991), Foley (1990), and even the edited volume published in tribute to Willis's work (Dolby and Dimitriadis 2004), takes up the central premises of production and reproduction and attempts to tweak them a bit theoretically—typically to add some possible evidence of human agency and the possibility for social and cultural change in the face of the basic theory's overwhelmingly determinist forces. The result of this process, as evidence collected across multiple sites and interpreted by multiple ethnographers engages the abstracted principles of social behavior, is an ever more updated, elaborated, refined, and robust general theory of how students' identities and futures are formed within the institution of the secondary school.

In many other areas of educational research, however, a study's research design and references to social theory and previous research are often not nearly as critical or skeptical in their relation to each other. For example, in an analysis I recently conducted of 69 studies in literacy research published in three major research journals that made substantial use of social theory in their research design and/or analysis of data (Dressman 2007), I found that in 60 of 69 studies, researchers seldom challenged any precepts of the social theories they referenced in their presentation of findings. In fact, in a plurality of cases (32), I found that the empirical findings of a study were used as illustrations of a theory's complete relevance in describing a social phenomenon. Researchers in these instances typically phrased relations between theory and their findings in terms such as "Participation... called attention to the hierarchical relationships among men, or what Connell (1987) referred to as the gender order" (Young 2000: 328); or, "As Lave and Wenger's (1991) theory would suggest..." (Prior 1995: 319).

As a consequence, many areas of social theory within educational research, such as social constructivism and Bakhtinian theories of language, get taken up and are uncritically applied to an ever expanding range of settings, but the validity of the theories is never examined, nor are theories ever expanded upon or reshaped through their engagement with empirical evidence. The uncritical use of social theory to warrant the arguments of much educational research has a number of implications, not only for the credibility of a study's findings but in the long term for the potential contribution of social theory to general bodies of knowledge about education.

Rick's reading in the sociology of secondary education widened and the questions his comparison of theory to his classroom experiences raised were partially addressed in the course he registered for in the next term, "Youth Cultures." The course examined the ways in which adolescents engaged not only schooling but other institutions in their lives, such as family and religion. Its major focus, however, was an examination of the ways in which adolescents related to the consumer items offered to them, such as clothes and music, and in particular to the communications revolution of cell phones, satellite television, and the Internet. The first assignment for the course was to gather information, either through interviews with individuals or through a survey, of a group of adolescents' tastes in music and fashion, and to determine what forms of electronic communication they used on a daily basis, how they accessed these forms, and why and how they used them. Rick decided to construct a survey and ask the students in his third period class—the class with the least apparent interest in history, and the class he struggled with most—to complete it for him. The students were very reluctant to cooperate at first, but the promise of anonymity, and, Rick suspected, the opportunity to "waste" the greater part of a class period, won them over.

Later at home, Rick was stunned by what the survey revealed about his students' use of electronic media. Of 26 students in the class, 20 owned a cell phone and claimed to use it on an "almost hourly" basis. How could that be? Rick wondered. Cell phones were banned at school. Sure, he'd caught a student or two in his class with a phone out, texting a message, but he'd never turned anyone in. A quick warning look and the student put the phone away; Rick figured that was enough to keep the situation under control. But 20 phones? An "almost hourly" basis? It didn't seem possible. He was just as astonished by what students reported about their use of satellite TV and the Internet. Eighteen students reported having satellite dishes in their homes and watching "international" programs—programs beamed in from outside the country, such as from China, Pakistan, or South Africa—on a nightly basis. Twenty-one claimed to spend an hour or more online every day. On a hunch, Rick logged-on to Facebook and typed in the names of several of his students, but nothing came up. Then he typed in a nickname that he'd heard one student call another. Instantly, the student's name and photograph came up. He tried another nickname, then another, with the same result.

The next day, Rick shared the findings of the survey with his students, and asked them to confirm that they'd been honest in their answers. The students seemed surprised that Rick was surprised. "Okay," said Rick. "Now, I'm going to ask for a show of hands. I'm not going to write anyone's name down or anything, so it's cool. I just want to know: How many of you have ever sent or received a text during this class?" Smiling coyly and looking at each other for support, 20 hands were slowly raised. "And, how many have sent or received a message during this class this week?" Nearly as many hands were raised. "Really?" asked Rick. "And how is it I don't see it?" Smiles all around, but silence. "Come on, I won't do anything; I just want to know. Ava? Peter? Shawntay?"

"Maybe," Shawntay smiled and said quietly, "It's because you're not looking."

Rick smiled but said nothing in response. "Okay, so tell me, and again, I won't write anything down, but I'm just curious: Who's got satellite TV at home?" Aakash, Ava, Xun, Angelina—nearly all the students who were immigrants or whose parents had immigrated—raised their hands. "And who's got a page on Facebook or MySpace?" Fifteen hands were raised. "Wow," said Rick.

"It's no big deal," Luis offered. "Everybody texts all the time. Everybody's on MySpace or Facebook. Everybody watches TV from back home. It's how we kill some time."

Rick's report mirrored the reports of several other students in his Youth Cultures course. Chris, a teacher at a school in the suburbs, reported that nearly 100 percent of her students claimed to spend "at least" two hours online each night, instant messaging friends and playing online video games with people around the world. Patti, who taught in a vocational-technical institute, reported that multiple students in her classes were deeply involved in online "virtual worlds" in which they had alternate identities, or maintained websites on topics that received thousands of hits per week. Edmund, who worked as a counselor at an urban youth center, reported that perhaps half the kids who came in had cell phones, but only a few said they spent "a lot of time online." Through cross-comparisons such as these, the students in the class, many of whom, like Rick, were in their late 20s and early 30s, slowly developed a picture of adolescent life that was very different from the youth culture of their own time, just 10–15 years earlier. It was a culture in which adolescents increasingly negotiated two parallel worlds, an "old" world of family, school, and birth culture that was bound by tradition, politics, and economics, and a "new" world, synthesized of electronically mediated pictures, sounds, and texts, that seemed unrestricted or at least not weighed down by history, politics, or even perhaps geography and economics.

The instructor for the course expanded on the students' observations in grand theoretical terms. This new world of electronic mediation was one in which adolescents were forging new relationships and new identities that offered possibilities for freedom from the restrictions of race, class, gender, and religion. Adolescents' use of ubiquitous electronic media had turned them into producers rather than mere consumers of goods and services and was preparing them for entry into the global economy as players rather than pawns. Against this new world, the one old could not compete, and was being left behind more than actively resisted.

"And the schools?" one student asked.

"You work in them," the instructor replied. "You see how students are acting. Secondary schools today are a ... a dead zone."

## The seductions of theory

The siren song of a good theory can be difficult to resist. Everyday the sun appears on one horizon, moves across the sky, and disappears on the opposite horizon. Is it not then completely reasonable to theorize that the sun revolves around the earth? The historian of science Thomas Kuhn (1996, first published 1962) argued that rather than proceeding in a fully rational manner, the evidence of history shows that what is held to be scientifically valid, or *paradigmatic*, about a phenomenon is the product of a highly social process whose practices are typically guided less by continual challenge than by general acceptance, and by activities meant to "mop up" (p. 24) after a theory until, at some point, that theory's contradictions become too great to explain away, and a revolutionary new theory takes its place. Over time and across multiple conversations, an ever more elaborated theory develops to explain (away) the incongruities between a theory's properties and anomalies, such as daily shifts in the point on the horizon where the sun rises and sets or the movement of stars and other planets in relation to the earth throughout the year. However, Kuhn also noted that "the state of Ptolemaic astronomy was a scandal before Copernicus' announcement" (p. 67). Well-entrenched theories often display a robust hold on a community of researchers that extends well beyond the presentation of disconfirming evidence. This is particularly the case when a theory becomes ingrained in the collective imagination of a culture, not merely as a plausible explanation but as the truth itself, and begins to appear as the physical manifestation of *metaphysical* realities—as the expression of people's deepest desires, such as the centrality of Earth and of human experience within God's plan for the universe.

So too, do social theories capture the desire of the people who weave them and use them within their academic communities to project a vision of a more just, more equitable, and more productive social world, one whose bright possibilities override any disconfirming evidence or alternate explanation. After several decades of debate about the extent to which secondary students might productively resist the forces of social and cultural reproduction, the advent of cheap and ubiquitous electronic media would appear the ultimate solution to this dilemma, one in which students' clever appropriations of technology triumph over those forces—indeed, over schooling itself, and perhaps more generally over the power of the state to regulate their lives (Appadurai 1996). As clearly as the sun rises and sets, adolescents' use of electronic media affords them a degree of virtual movement across space and time and the latitude to construct a persona, if not a full identity, that is different from the one family and society have given them. And so it is theorized that the world as it previously existed will change, too— or be left behind, and with it, its intractable social and cultural problems.

Separation of human social behavior from the social beings who study it has been so difficult to achieve and theories of the social have been so multiple and so interwoven with their historical and cultural contexts that, from a Kuhnian perspective, the social sciences are sometimes referred to as "pre-paradigmatic" in their approaches (Kuhn 1996: 15). Other philosophers and historians of science such as Longino (1990) and Gould (1996), however, have noted the extent to which human social values have inflected the study of human biology from early modern times into the present. Similarly, the continual interplay among multiple cosmological (observationally based) and cosmonological (more speculative) theories of the universe and its origins also challenges whether the "normal (natural) sciences," as Kuhn called them, are untouched by human subjectivity, particularly with respect to grand questions that touch on the meaning of human experience and existence.

The tendency for theories of any sort to become regarded by their users as objective statements of fact was so troublesome to the philosopher

Ludwig Wittgenstein that he routinely railed against theorizing as a practice within any form of inquiry (Monk 1990). Instead, Wittgenstein advocated that phenomena be described in the plainest language possible, in terms that were stripped of all interpretation. Only then, through the cross-comparison of plainly described cases guided by relentless skepticism, could researchers and philosophers begin to name and understand phenomena with clarity. Wittgenstein's prescription, however, was an extreme solution that, I would argue, contradicts itself (since it and much of Wittgenstein's work is itself highly theoretical in nature) and that lacks practical awareness of the extent to which even the plainest language is ridden with inescapable assumptions and presumptions that are very well hidden from even the most self-honest and skeptical of inquirers.

Moreover and as I have argued in earlier chapters, as sources of counterintuitive explanations of everyday experiences, social theories are invaluable "lenses," or devices for seeing the world afresh, for articulating creative and original (if also untried) responses to intractable social problems, and, as Kuhn also pointed out, for providing a community of researchers with a common discourse and set of assumptions—a framework, or paradigm—on which, until a more comprehensive theory is developed, understanding might be extended and refined. To ignore or avoid social theory in one's approach to educational research in a Wittgensteinian attempt to avoid "bewitchment" (Brenner 1999: 7) is neither feasible nor advisable. A better and more practical approach may be to attend to a "weaker," less exacting interpretation of Wittgenstein's argument, by remaining in a state of continual skepticism and self-examination about one's use of and attraction to a particular social theory as a sense-making framework, and by applying different theoretical frameworks to the same experience and comparing and contrasting among them.

Although these issues may seem esoteric and beyond the ken of a researcher in either the early stages of a research project or her career, to proceed without continually questioning the validity of a theoretical framework and its applicability to the situation under investigation is to invite two outcomes that, in turn, may have serious consequences (1) for the credibility of one's work; (2) more generally, for the credibility of research that uses social theoretical frameworks; and (3) for the study's potential contribution to the construction of a body of general knowledge about a phenomenon. One likely outcome of a slavish devotion to a particular theoretical frame is the premature foreclosure of possible sources and types of data or analytical techniques, such as coding practices, that can significantly limit the range of possible interpretations of data in later stages of a study.

A possible second, related outcome is the substitution of theory for evidence, where data is missing, in order to make a claim. For example, lacking tangible historical evidence of experiences or details of a student's educational history that would explain her or his behavior in the present, a researcher may believe and argue that they must have occurred or exist because that would be consistent with his theoretical framework. Thus, a child's precocious use of language might be explained as the result of earlier undocumented experiences with books, described in terms whose details are largely the product of the researcher's imaginative and enamored reading of Bakhtin (1981); or, a student's unwarranted designation as learning disabled might be attributed, without concrete evidence, to presumed discursive and regulatory practices that only a Foucauldian (Foucault 1977) framework would explain.

In the case of either outcome, the credibility of a study's claims would likely be dismissed by other researchers. A critical examination of the study's arguments could easily lead to the conclusion that instead of "mopping up" or further explicating a theoretical framework, the researcher had "found what he was looking for," or worse yet, that he had simply invented it. Beyond challenging the internal validity and credibility of an individual study's claims, however, these outcomes can also have a general negative effect on the significance of social theoretical research for policy making. In the United States, at least, qualitative research studies, and in particular those that make substantial use of "exotic" social theories such as the ones described in this book, have struggled to respond to charges that they lack "objectivity" and "generalizability," and therefore that their findings can and should have no impact on the making of educational policy or on curricular and instructional reforms (Shavelson and Towne 2002). The reasons behind these charges are complex and have as much to do with politics as with epistemological issues; still, inappropriate uses of social theory to make research-based arguments can only damage the credibility and impact of social theoretical research within the policy arena. But even if researchers who use social theory to frame their work renounce any interest in influencing policy and choose instead to justify their practices as contributing to their field's knowledge base, the consequences of using social theories in uncritical ways or in substitution for missing evidence in an argument can only weaken the discursive coherence of conversations within an area of educational research. In my opinion, this may be the direst consequence of all of an overzealous use of social theory.

Given these challenges, a more advisable approach to using social theory might be to refrain from making it a part of one's process until after data has been collected and analyzed; indeed, in his influential book on critical ethnographic methods in education, Carspecken (1996) does not advocate the use of social theory until the final, interpretive stages of the research process. In my experience, however, waiting until the very late stages of a research project, or even until the "writing up" of findings, often leads to a rather superficial, after-the-fact use of social theory that typically makes only very limited use of theory as a framework for building knowledge, and seldom if ever contributes to the refinement of the theory itself. Moreover, since researchers who use social theory in their work are typically well-read in a particular theory *before* they begin a research project, refraining from explicitly using that theory from the start of a project only increases the likelihood of its implicit, unexamined influence on the development of research questions, design, and data collection and analysis. In the end, I would suggest that an explicit but ever-critical use of social theory, or perhaps even the comparative application of multiple social theories from the early stages of a project onward, is the approach most likely to produce findings that make the most complete and most valid use of social theory, and that in turn are the most likely to contribute reflexively to the refinement of theory itself.

Over the next several weeks, Rick continued to compare the readings and discussions from his Youth Cultures course to his observations of student activity on an almost daily basis. In the wake of the "outing" of his students' in-class texting, a few had tried openly to use their cell phones; but Rick feared the direction this would take his class and clamped down on this activity, at least in the open. His report of these events fueled much discussion in Youth Cultures about the *liminality* (McLaren 1986; see also Turner 1969) of students' resistance and teachers' complicity in much of it. Rick found these analyses intriguing, but he wasn't totally convinced by them. Explanations of each incident in his and others' interactions with adolescents seemed too easy to come by, too facile for him. And, he continued to wonder what the implications of this theoretical analysis were for teaching his subject matter, since it seemed that actually *learning* anything—that is, anything of academic significance—was beside the point within their discussion.

As the midpoint of the semester drew near, discussion turned to the final research project, which was to involve analysis of systematically collected data from course participants' worksites. Some individuals were planning interviews with adolescents and perhaps even some visits to their homes. The instructor for the course suggested that Rick might want to conduct a cross-case analysis of students who were immigrants, native born but from immigrant parents, and those whose families had lived in the country for several generations. Rick considered this idea, but again he wondered what connection it would have to teaching his subject, which he continued to regard as the "real" raison d'etre for his classroom and his career.

And then, Tom's older brother Evan was killed in Afghanistan. The news shook the school, for Evan had graduated from there only a few years before. Rick hadn't taught Evan, but as a star on the school's football team he'd certainly known of him and of his athletic prowess and status as one of the school's student leaders. But, strangely, Rick didn't know that Evan had joined the Army or that he was in Afghanistan. Tom was a quiet student and had never mentioned it.

In the week surrounding the return of Evan's body and the funeral, very little was accomplished at school in the way of instruction. Emotions among the students were strong. Many other students had connections with military personnel serving in the Middle East and Afghanistan, and of these, a number were close relatives. There were several assemblies and a memorial service, and teachers were encouraged to allow time for students to talk through their feelings about Evan and the circumstances of his death. When Rick asked his students to write an essay in class one day about what they were feeling and thinking, they were some of the longest responses to a writing prompt he had ever received. Rick also noted that the students' essays were more varied in their points of view than were comments made in class discussions. In their writing, several students expressed outrage at their government's participation in the conflict at all. Others did not defend the nation's involvement, but the emotional tone of remarks about 9/11, Islam and terrorism, and "turban heads who treat their women like crap" implied their tacit support for the war. The language of this latter group alarmed Rick. He supposed that it accounted for the lack of participation in class discussions by the students in his class who were Muslim, or even from the Asian students, for that matter, and also for the defensive tone of those students' essays. His suspicions were confirmed a few days later when Sanjay, with whom he was close, complained to Rick that he'd been jostled in the hallway and called a "turban head" by two older students not in Rick's class. "I'm not even Muslim," Sanjay said. "I'm Hindu. My parents came from India, *but I was born in this country!* Don't they know the difference?!" Then Sanjay told him that some other students who were Muslim had been threatened but were afraid to report it.

Rick's frustration boiled over later that evening in his Youth Cultures course after his fellow students began to "theorize" Rick's telling of the day's events. "I don't see what difference theorizing makes for my students and my classroom," he snapped in exasperation. "It's easy to sit back and explain it all away *after it happens*. But what does your 'theory' have to say about how to stop this nonsense?! Maybe school is a wasteland and the kids are all bored to death. But I've got a problem and I need a solution, not another 'problematization!'"

The class grew silent after Rick's last remark. Then Edmund spoke. "Well," he ventured, "It sounds to me like your students are finally *not* bored by school."

"Yeah, you've got a real tiger by the tail there," Sheila, a teacher at a neighboring school, added. "So, what can you do about it ... well, it seems to me that what you need is a way for all your students to have a voice in this, you know, like maybe you could start a blog and have the students comment on it."

"Or maybe," the instructor for the course suggested, "You could have different groups of students produce videos about how they see the world and their place in it."

"Yeah, you could call it *The War at Home*," Chris suggested.

"And it could be your research project for this course," the instructor added.

Over the next week Rick consulted with the technology specialist at his school and discovered how relatively simple digital video production was and that the school had just purchased several cameras he could use. The instructor for the course was enthusiastic about the project, and urged Rick "to do it right"—that is, to be systematic in recording the events of the project as it progressed, collecting artifacts, including his own as well as the students' points of view, and checking his perceptions against the students' as well as against outsiders' interpretations of the evidence collected. Over the next two weeks, the instructor outlined the basics of qualitative research design for the students, and met with them to generate research questions and modes of data collection and analysis that would provide an empirical foundation for their theoretical analyses.

Rick's plan called for the students in his third period class to organize themselves into groups of four or five students and to choose a topic and approach to studying the impact of the conflicts in Afghanistan and the Middle East on the school and the community. He estimated that the students should take one week of class time to plan the video, two weeks to research and shoot it, and three weeks to edit and polish the final project. These would then be compiled as a series of video segments and would be shown at an evening assembly that would be open to parents, students, and teachers in the school. With the theoretical framework of the course in mind, Rick worked back and forth between the issues of resistance and engagement that he was struggling with in his own teaching, and practical issues of what and how much data he could reasonably and reliably collect in the six weeks that had been allotted for data collection in the project. After several rounds of writing and revising following feedback from other students in his course and the instructor, Rick generated four research questions that were informed by his reading of theory and his own teaching experiences and that could be answered through an analysis of the data he would be able to collect:

1  Will the video project increase students' engagement with course content? If so, how?
2  Will the students' social and cultural backgrounds be reflected in project decisions? If so, how?
3  What sources of information and images will students draw from in their projects?
4  What differences will be seen across groups in the content and style of the students' final video products?

Some of his peers wondered if Rick's fourth question wasn't a subquestion of his second, and should be included with it. Rick considered this option, but decided in the end that a focus on a comparison of the final video products across groups could be significant enough to deserve its own analytical focus.

With the admonition of the instructor in mind that it was better to collect data from a few sources rigorously than to collect data from a lot of sources in a scattered and haphazard fashion, Rick decided that over the six-week period he could reasonably keep field notes during class and write more extended reflections several evenings a week; require students to log their activities for the day in the last five minutes of each class meeting; collect all the students raw footage and final videos; and interview each group of students twice, once at the three-week mark, and once after they had completed their videos. Rick had originally planned to interview each student before and after the project was completed, but realized that he would not be able to conduct, transcribe, and analyze 52 separate interviews within the time frame of the project.

In the last stage of design, each student in the Youth Cultures course was presented with a matrix, or chart in grid format. Down the left column of the matrix, the students wrote one research question in each cell of the column; across the top row, the students listed one form of data to be collected. They then filled in the grid to describe the analytical practices, such as coding (marking the patterns or recurring terms or ideas in transcripts or other artifacts) and comparing and contrasting different samples of data. This preliminary plan for data analysis was to be both specific in terms of the types of possible coding schemes and comparisons and contrasts to be made and open to possible unexpected patterns and themes that might occur. The preliminary plan that Rick presented in class just prior to the beginning of his data collection is shown in Table 3.1.

## Theoretically framing research practices

One of the great challenges of qualitative and ethnographic research, particularly when it is conducted on a small scale over a limited period of time by a single researcher, is finding a balance between how much and what kind of data can be collected, and what it is reasonably possible to collect, given the practical limitations of time and access to what participants are thinking, feeling, and doing, both in the moment and later, upon reflection. Ideally, the answer to the question of what should be collected within a specific cultural context is: Everything. Practically, that is not possible, not only because a single individual could not possibly record every remark and action made by participants within a field of investigation, as well as record their reflections on every aspect of a project and all details of the setting, but also because the time and energy required afterward to transcribe, code, and distill that much data into a single representation of a series of events is typically not available to an individual researcher (or even, for that matter, to a team of researchers).

Table 3.1 Rick's research questions, data sources, and preliminary plan for analysis

| Research question | Data source | | | |
|---|---|---|---|---|
| | Field notes (kept by Rick) | Student activity logs (kept by Students) | Two open-ended, audio-taped interviews with student groups | Video footage (raw footage and final, edited video) |
| 1. Will the video project increase students' engagement with course content? If so, how? | Code for evidence of resistance, engagement, or other possible factors | Code for consistency and (in)congruence with my field notes; categorize student comments about process and progress | Transcribe and code for issues raised by students and for evidence of resistance and/or engagement | Code for length, quantity of footage, and for style and creativity of the final product |
| 2. Will the students' social and cultural backgrounds be reflected in project decisions? If so, how? | Code for references to gender, religion, politics, race, social class, or other possible markers of difference | Code for possible references to gender, religion, ethnicity, politics, race, social class, or other possible markers | Code for references to gender, religion, ethnicity, politics, race, social class, or other possible markers of difference | Code for gender, religion, ethnicity, politics, race, social class, or other markers in raw footage and final videos |
| 3. What sources of information and images will students draw from in their projects? | Record students' use of the Internet and other data sources, as well as list subjects of video shooting | Instruct students to identify and record all sources of info they use on a daily basis; compare their records to lists from my field notes | Check sources with students during interviews; ask about reasoning processes for finding and using these sources | Identify and inventory all audio and visual images and information sources in the final video products |
| 4. What differences will be seen across groups in the content and style of their final video product? | Not applicable | Not applicable | Ask groups to compare and contrast their videos with other groups; code transcripts for differences identified by the groups | Code for content and stylistic markers; compare and contrast across groups |

From the start, then, one should develop a clear rationale about what data sources are and are not needed to address specific research questions, and how that data can be reliably collected and organized. Having a clearly developed theoretical framework and a clearly developed position with respect to how a theory and related previous research may inform the analysis of data can be an enormous advantage in this respect, because of the focus that a theoretical framework brings to the development—the narrowing down—of research questions. Once clear research questions have been composed, it should be relatively simple to ask what kinds of data will be needed to answer them, and then to ask how large the sample will need to be to obtain data in which recurrent patterns and possible exceptions to these patterns can be made evident, and whether and how it might be possible to collect the data in a regular, systematic fashion.

Although a full discussion of ethnographic and qualitative methodology is beyond the scope of this book (for that, I recommend Carspecken 1996), I will offer a few practical tips. First, in my experience, field notes taken in situ as events are unfolding are often the greatest source of insight when reconstructing events for analysis and the writing up of findings. Carrying a clipboard or a notepad may seem awkward or intrusive in some circumstances, but there are ways to keep writing materials close at hand and quickly jot down notes or comments, or simply to remove oneself to a corner and quickly sketch a scene in words. These notes can then be used for reconstructing a fuller account at a later time in far greater detail and with much greater accuracy than if one relied on memory alone, and for the writing of longer, more reflective field notes at the end of the day or week. In some cases where permission has been obtained, audio and/or video recordings can also be made, but these cannot be relied upon as the sole record, since camera angles can obscure as well as reveal behavior and voices that are sometimes unclear or can't be sorted out when multiple participants speak at once.

Second, interviews are vital sources of information, and are a necessity when checking the accuracy of a researcher's interpretation of events or what a participant may have meant by a particular statement, but they are seldom sufficient sources of information by themselves (for an excellent discussion of these issues, see Atkinson *et al.* 2003). Moreover, they can be very time consuming, both for participants and for the researcher, who will also need to transcribe or arrange for the transcription of tapes afterwards, and are often socially awkward. Again, in my experience, focus group interviews conducted with groups of four or five participants are often more efficient and also produce richer information, particularly if the interview is conducted as a conversation in which participants speak freely, although individual interviews with key participants are also important.

Third, it is crucial to collect full sets of whatever artifacts might be related to one's inquiry. Photocopies of documents and photographs of objects should be made and labeled. There are legal and ethical issues associated with photographing participants, particularly children, but it is typically not difficult to obtain permission to photograph classrooms, bulletin boards, or other public spaces. In addition, where the space in which events occur is also critical, as in a classroom or a library, it may be very useful to draw a map of the space and the objects within it, for later reference and analysis.

Fourth and finally, sometimes it can be useful to ask participants to self-report on their activities, as a means of *triangulating*, or corroborating, one's own records, or comparing one's own perception of events with participants'. However, no matter how well intentioned, participants may often forget to do so or may try to recall what they did days after it has happened, with resulting inaccuracies.

As research questions develop and the data to be collected are identified, to keep relations among questions, data, and analysis coherent and focused I would recommend that a chart similar to the one in Table 3.1 be constructed, with data sources listed along the top row and research questions down the side. This will allow a researcher to specify which sources of data will address which research questions. It is also the point at which, in a preliminary and open-ended way, processes and categories of analysis can be named. However, it is important to remember that at this stage of the research, these processes and categories are tentative and open to revision. Unlike experimental research designs, in which conditions are tightly controlled in the expectation that a rather precise set of outcomes may be produced, qualitative and ethnographic research presumes that in a naturalistic setting, outcomes cannot always be so carefully predicted. Indeed, qualitative and ethnographic research assumes that the unpredictable is as critical and as "normative" a part of human experience as the predictable, and that the unexpected can reveal more of the underlying dynamics of a social situation than what is normatively taken for granted. The researcher who plans carefully but who remains flexible and open to odd twists and unpredicted turns will collect data that is far more comprehensive and will produce findings that are truer to the complexity of human society and culture than the researcher who allows his or her reading of the literature and predetermined plan to produce a predetermined set of findings.

The students in Rick's third-period class were alternately intrigued and skeptical about the video project Rick proposed to them. When he suggested they could form their own groups and choose the people they would interview and the direction their 5–10-minute segment would take, Sylvia, who was Deidre's best friend and who had a reputation for bluntness, asked, "What? You mean you aren't going to tell us what to say?"

"No," Rick said. "Of course, you can't insult anyone, and you need to be responsible about what you say—you have to back your opinions up with facts."

"That's what I thought," Sylvia snickered.

But other students were less cynical. Sanjay was very enthusiastic, and joined with Aakash and two boys from Muslim families, Dris and Fazal, to produce a video segment that they said would tell the other side of the politics of the conflict, to be titled "Justice for All." They asked Ava to join them, but she chose to work with Deidre, Sylvia, Angelina, and Shawntay on a segment to be titled "Girls in War." Darren and Luis teamed up with Rosa and Lisa to interview members of their respective Black, Latino and Asian communities for a segment tentatively titled "Whose War Is It?" Another group, composed of Peter and four White males, proposed to interview teachers and administrators at school for a segment they would call "Support Our Troops." Rick helped to organize several other students form groups to produce two videos. One would consist of interviews with people at large in the community and be called "Public Opinion"; the other would interview students and be called "Student Perspectives." After class, Tom, who had just returned to school and had not joined any group, approached Rick. Rick told him that he could do a project on his own in the library, if he preferred. But Tom rejected the suggestion, and asked instead if he could make a video "on my own." Rick agreed.

Rick thought that the project was off to a good start, and recorded his impressions along with an account of how the groups had formed in his field notes. Later that evening, he reported his experiences in a meeting with Edmund, Chris, and Sheila, the members of his Youth Cultures study group, at a local pub. Chris thought the grouping of some of the students by gender and general cultural affiliation, and the selection of topics that seemed, predictably, to reflect the perspectives of these groups on the conflict, ought to generate some interesting data for analysis.

But over the next few days as Rick worked with the groups to develop a plan for their videos, enthusiasm seemed to wane. He sent the members of the Public Opinion group off to the computer lab to search for websites on the

Internet with different points of view about the conflict, but when he checked on them toward the end of the class session, he found that the students had struggled with the search engines and the sheer volume of information available, and had identified very few sites. The Girls in War group spent much of a class period discussing the topic, but in the end identified only two people they wanted to interview. The Justice for All group were motivated, but argued over the point of view the video should have, and made little progress. Rick conscientiously reported these events in his field notes and shared his growing frustration with the study group at their next meeting. Sheila wondered if Rick was not pushing the students too hard to plan in advance. "Yeah, maybe you should just give them the cameras and get out of the way," Chris suggested.

Rick also wondered if he was interfering too much in the students' work by making the project seem too much like any other assignment. The students had to be prodded to complete the daily logs of their activity; they filled them in as briefly as possible and sometimes inaccurately. As a way of rekindling interest, on Monday he brought several video cameras to class, demonstrated briefly how to use them, and then gave cameras to the Support Our Troops, Girls in War, and Student Perspectives groups and told them to "find a quiet place" in the school and practice interviewing each other. With three groups on their own, he sat down to encourage and offer support and ideas to the other groups, but without, he hoped, pressuring them or interfering.

The next day, Rick opened class by asking the three groups who had practiced with the cameras before if the class could view some of the footage they'd shot. The groups seemed surprised by this but without further discussion, Rick put the Girls in War tape in a camera that was connected to a television and pressed "Play." Ten minutes followed of the girls' hand-held shots of asking other girls around the school their opinions about the war, with little or no response from the interviewees. Undaunted, Rick played the Student Perspectives group's tape, but it consisted largely of shots of the students interviewing each other that were out of focus, that were backlit and showed only the speaker's shadow, or with unintelligible sound. After a few minutes of this, Rick stopped the tape and reached for the Support Our Troops tape. "Uh, Mr. C—" Peter stammered. But it was too late. In the opening scene of the tape, the camera moved down the hall, paused at the boy's lavatory, and then entered. Inside, the camera moved to a stall door; a hand reached out and knocked. The door slowly swung open, and Curtis, one of the group, was seen sitting on the toilet with his pants half-down. The students screamed, laughed, and hooted.

"And sir, can you tell us what you think of the Taliban?" Peter's voice asked.

"The Taliban?! I'll tell you what I think of the Taliban," Curtis shouted, as he stood up, turned around, and mooned the camera. "They can kiss my arse!"

Rick wrote later in his field notes that the screams of laughter gave him time to consider his response, which he decided could not be of the anger and disappointment he was feeling. They'd gotten him again, but he couldn't show it. "Very 'cheeky,'" he said when the laughter had subsided. "But listen, we're going to show these videos to anyone who wants to come and see them in less than five weeks. And is this the kind of stuff you want people to see?"

In the following days, the students seemed to settle down to work. Rick decided that he would not release cameras to students until they could show him a clear plan for shooting, complete with a short script and shot angles. These plans were slow to generate, but with much prodding and a few revision sessions, by the end of two weeks nearly every group had completed a few minutes of taping.

But the atmosphere of the class once again seemed joyless. Midway through the third week, Rick met again with his study group and bemoaned the project's lack of progress. "It's just like before," he said. "I see the same lack of engagement with this project, the same resistance to just about everything I try, that I've seen all year long. These kids are just slackers, that's all."

## Theory and the unexpected

Although it may seem overly homiletic, it is often when the interplay between social theory and empirical evidence produces a great deal of friction—when one's theoretically informed expectations are not met by experience, often to one's great frustration—that, ironically, the greatest theoretical insights and the deepest understanding of a situation may be generated. Many years ago, I conducted a comparative analysis of how primary school children in three schools that served students from very different socioeconomic and ethnic backgrounds made sense of their school library's organizational structure (Dressman 1997). As part of my data collection, I showed focus groups of students in each school 35 books and periodicals that were representative of the range of texts in their libraries, and asked them to sort them into categories "that made sense" to them and to give each a name. I expected that students in the upper-class school, who were above grade level in achievement and whose parents typically possessed advanced professional degrees, would develop highly creative categories of organization, against the order of the library; but I was wrong. The students in the upper-class school organized the books into groups that mirrored the conventional organization of the library, while students in the working-class school developed highly creative categories that were unconventional but nonetheless well-reasoned. This finding was very surprising to me. However, looking back over other data, I realized that a theme of conformity to conventional expectations ran throughout the data for the upper-class school, while in the working-class school, students were taught "the rules," but were not sanctioned for making sense of information on their own terms. The result was an analysis in which I "interrogated" the assumptions of social class privilege, arguing that the students in the upper-class school were by no means any more "free" by virtue of their superior material and test-proved academic superiority, than were working-class students who lacked material and academic advantage, but were able to construct the library on their own terms.

So, too, in the example of Rick's students' video project, events are challenging the dichotomy between resistance and engagement that Rick has set up through his reading of social and cultural theories of reproduction and production, and his course readings on youth culture and electronically mediated forms of literacy. Can students both resist and engage school assignments at the same time? If so, what does it mean to "resist?" What are its outward signs, and do these correspond to inward resistance? Are electronic literacies so simple and effortless in their practices production and consumption that they effectively eliminate the former challenges of print-only literacy? And, what of the multiple political layers of this project, of the consciousness of the students that they are not simply fulfilling a school assignment with their video making, but also making a statement of their own identity and place in the world that will be made visible to their families and community?

At the end of three weeks, Rick was very concerned that any of the group's video segments would be completed on time. He had raised the idea of a public viewing of the video with his school director, who had approved the plan, provided that he was able to preview the entire product a week before it was shown. Rick was certain the videos would not be ready by then, and negotiated a compromise: a private viewing in the evening for teachers and the students' family and friends. Rick hoped this would take some of the pressure off the students, but when he announced the plan, the students balked. "You mean you want my *father* to see this?" Aakash asked nervously.

Surprisingly, when Rick conducted his first round of focus interviews with each group and asked how the students thought their videos were coming along, few expressed concern. "We'll get it done," Angelina promised. "You know, this is harder than it looks. There are a lot of things you have to think about, and something always goes wrong, but we'll get it done."

By Week Four, some groups had completed several video shoots, while other groups, Public Opinion in particular, had completed very little. Rick recorded his resignation that the project might not be completed in his field notes, but he couldn't wait for everyone to catch up. He selected one volunteer from each group and took them to the computer lab for two days' tutorial in digital video editing. "Now, you are the lead editor for your group," he told the students. "It's all up to you now." At the end of the day he was amazed when he passed by the computer lab on his way out the door and saw not only every student in the tutoring group but several of their classmates as well, huddled around the monitors. "Mr. C., come here a minute," Darren called. "Look at this!" Darren clicked a tab on the monitor screen and hip-hop blared from the speakers, followed by the panning image of a graffiti-covered wall that read, in spay-painted letters more than a meter high, "Whose War Is It?" Darren and his group members grinned and danced to the music. "Sweet, huh? That's all we've got so far."

Over the next two and a half weeks, the computer lab was filled with students every evening after school, composing and editing their video segment. Not all the students in Rick's class stayed late, but Rick cajoled the technology coordinator to let him move his class to the lab, and enough students stayed late each night that each segment slowly began to take form. Tom was particularly focused on his project. He sat alone at the computer for hours at a time, rarely asking for help. On several occasions Rick sat with Tom and saw that he was using very little video footage; instead, Tom was weaving family photos and images he'd downloaded from the Internet into a statement about his brother's life.

At the end of Week Five, Rick was confident enough to send a message home to parents and announce to the students and faculty that the video project would have its premier next Thursday evening. With this news, the students scrambled to re-shoot some footage with poor lighting or unintelligible sound and to complete soundtracks, voice-over narrations, and titling. With editing continuing into late Thursday afternoon, it was decided that the segments would be shown individually, and in no particular sequence, except for Tom's segment, which he had asked to go last.

Only a few parents and teachers attended the premiere that night, but nearly all the students and many of their friends were there. Each video segment, Rick wrote in his field notes afterwards, expressed the distinctive cultural and political views of the groups, but seemed also to draw stylistically from a single bank of adolescent pop cultural television and music video techniques. The segments were both slick and amateur and, most telling, he thought, they lacked any real evidence of research, or ... or, substance, he wrote.

But Rick's instructor and peers in his Youth Cultures course had a very different reading of the videos when he showed them for his final presentation. "Are you kidding?" Sheila asked, when Rick noted their lack of substance. "All semester long you've been describing these students as 'slackers,' but what I see is ... some very clever students using some really clever devices to say things that are really quite provocative, given their own cultural backgrounds and the politics of that school." Rick's instructor agreed, and after the class meeting pulled Rick aside to ask him if he'd been collecting all the data he'd planned to collect. Rick said yes, he had, but he still needed to conduct a follow-up round of focus interviews with each group. "That's fantastic," the instructor replied. Then he invited Rick to "write up" his findings as a chapter in an edited book he was putting together with the working title, "Youth Cultures in Tomorrow's Schools."

## Summary and conclusion

This chapter's focus has been on the use of social theory as a tool for conceptualizing and designing small-scale educational research projects, as illustrated by the fictional portrait of Rick Chavez, a teacher of modern history in a secondary school with a very diverse student population. The purpose of this fictional portrait was to lend a concrete dimension to the discussion of the theoretical and practical challenges to conceptualizing, designing, and implementing a research project that makes complex use of social theory. Rick's enrollment in two university courses served as the narrative vehicle for explicating the development of a long line of social theory and research in secondary education. In a parallel discussion of the role of theory within scientific inquiry and its implications for the theorization and research of human social behavior, I intended Rick's ambivalent, critical stance toward social theory as he applied it to the analysis of his own professional experience to serve as a model by which researchers might alternately apply and reciprocally critique and build upon the insights of social theories in their work.

The death of one of Rick's students' brothers in Afghanistan served as a narrative device whereby the permeation of classrooms by global and national events, as well as by students' cultural backgrounds, and the theoretical and pedagogical implications of this permeation could be fore grounded. It also provided a context for the design and implementation of a research project, and served to illustrate the messiness, but also the extraordinary generativity, of naturalistic social research that is informed by social theory and personal experience.

It might also be construed from this chapter that the conceptualization and design of a research project that uses social theory is largely a personal, subjective encounter between a researcher's lived experience and her or his reading of social theory, and one in which the perspectives of others matter only to the extent that the researcher judges them helpful. However, for a researcher's efforts to have an impact beyond her or his personal understanding requires the comparison and contrast of evidence with theory within discourses that are far more public, and that demand simultaneous attention both to the researcher's own reasoning processes and to the reasoning and rhetorical sensibilities of her or his prospective audience. Because he planned carefully and was consistent in his data collection practices, Rick Chavez is well-positioned to enter the discourses of research and theory. Yet, much analysis remains to be done, multiple arguments remain to be formed and tested, and the stylistic and rhetorical conventions of educational research remain to be acquired. The next chapter takes up the discussion of these three topics and their coordination, as Rick analyzes his data and writes up his findings for publication.

# Chapter 4

# Writing with social theory

## What's wrong with my theory?

A great advantage of having a well-developed theoretical framework before one begins analyzing data and writing up a research project is the direction and focus theory can give to these processes. To understand how this is so, imagine the collection and analysis of data for a study without an explicit theoretical perspective—for example, a study of the interactions among a teacher and students in a primary-level classroom. Without the directive focus of a theoretical framework, what data would need to be collected? Everything? But, what would constitute "everything" in this case? Would it include a written transcript of everything the teacher and students said to each other? Or, would it require audio capture of voices as well, to record tone, timing, pitch, accent, and the like? What of gestures? Perhaps video capture would also be needed. And, what of the conversations students had with each other, simultaneous with the teacher's talk? What of announcements over the school intercom? What of the language of written texts used during interactions, or of visual images, or other sounds? And, once "everything" had been collected, where and how would the analysis begin? How would a researcher begin to organize the data, to know what likely patterns to look for, and to recognize patterns that were unlikely? What would determine what was considered "likely" or "unlikely?" What would constitute a pattern? For that matter, where would the very idea of looking for "patterns" come from?

Studies such as the one above have been conducted, of course, particularly in the early years of classroom research, often under the rubrics of "exploration" and "objectivity." Still other studies have grounded their designs and analytical practices in previous research that was also supposedly a-theoretical and objective. However, the findings and conclusions drawn from studies such as these may not result, as Wittgenstein (1953) supposed, in seeing things afresh, but more often for researchers lacking

Wittgenstein's gifts for ruthless skepticism and relentless logic, in the application of their own tacit prejudices to the design, analysis, and interpretation of their data. Moreover, sometimes the consequences of these studies can be quite harmful, not only to the validity of researchers' claims but more significantly to teachers and students (see Labov 1972 and Dressman 1999; also Chapter Two, for two cases of researcher bias and their implications).

In contrast, imagine a study of classroom interactions framed, for example, by a reading of the work (and previous research based on) the Russian literary and language theorist, Mikhail Bakhtin (1981). A researcher who had self-consciously decided to use Bakhtin's work as a frame would have a very clear idea of what data should be collected, how to organize it, and what likely and unlikely patterns of interaction to observe. Bakhtin would also give the interpretation of the findings from the study a direction and focus. However, one criticism could be that in taking a Bakhtinian focus, other salient patterns or ways of framing the analysis and interpretation of events would be left unexamined and unaccounted for. The response to this challenge would be that the intent of this analysis was not to describe all aspects of a phenomenon as complex as classroom interactions are, and that the study was instead intended to focus on one aspect and to act as a complement to other analyses conducted using other theoretical perspectives.

A far more serious challenge, however, would be that the adoption of a Bakhtinian perspective without due consideration of its point of origin (the Soviet Union at the height of Stalinism) and its distance from contemporary classroom settings had led to an analysis and interpretation of data that was more distorted than focused, or alternately that the findings of the study and Bakhtin's theory seemed so congruent that the research appeared to have been contrived to illustrate the theory—that is, that the researcher was used by, rather than made use of, theory. Either of these challenges, if documented, would be very difficult to respond to after the fact, and would significantly reduce, if not invalidate, a study's contribution to the research literature.

The best hedge against this challenge is to turn relations between one's theoretical framework and one's data inside-out as early as possible within the research process. In other words, questions such as, "How does Bakhtin *not* explain my data?" and "What patterns or other evidence can I find in my data that challenge or contradict what Bakhtin would predict?" or even "What problems with or holes in Bakhtinian theory do the data suggest?" are as critical to ask as "How would Bakhtin explain these events?" or "What patterns reflect Bakhtin's descriptions of carnival, heteroglossia, and dialogism?" Negative questions about the applicability of a theory within a study should be raised during the development of research questions, but they are absolutely crucial, and are likely to be more specific in their focus and so have greater impact, during the analytical and interpretive phases of the research process.

Although I have described this strategy as a "hedge" against challenges to the validity of a theoretical analysis, I do not mean to suggest that it is merely a rhetorical ploy to make a researcher seem more self-critical than she or he actually is. Very often in quantitative and sometimes qualitative research, the "limitations" of a study are described in a section at the conclusion of a research article, such as its limited applicability to other settings, or anomalies in sampling or data collection and analysis. Without challenging their sincerity or candor, these discussions typically appear after-the-fact of the presentation of the study itself and often seem perfunctory. In Toulminian (1958) terms, a short qualification of claims followed by a rebuttal is not what I am suggesting. Rather, I am arguing for a thoroughly critical stance toward social theory, one that interrogates theory's capacity to serve as a warrant for data-based claims, and that begins as early as possible within the research process.

There is one final advantage that seeking the negation of one's theoretical framework as deliberately as its validation brings, and that is the creation of a "third place"—a position or point of view—that escapes the pitfalls and challenges of a research position grounded in the dubious claims of either subjectivity ("my point of view is as valid as anyone else's") or objectivity ("I'm just reporting the facts"). It is as though, rhetorically and epistemologically, in the tension between one's own point of view and "the facts," one has brought in a third party—a mediator—whom one does not trust completely, either. Representing as candidly as possible the interplay among these three agents—the researcher, the data, and theory—then becomes the goal of analyzing, interpreting, and writing up one's data for a potential audience of peers who are equally acquainted with the theoretical, analytic, and rhetorical practices in play.

A week after the close of the school year, Rick returned to his field notes, student logs, focus interviews, and the unedited footage and final versions of each group's video segment, and began to sift slowly through the material, in search of ... of what?, he wondered. Two months before, he had almost persuaded himself that the making of a video about the conflicts in Afghanistan and the Middle East would re-energize his teaching and his students' learning. But three weeks of little progress and student clowning followed by three weeks of messing around with editing software and some final projects which, while clever and distinctive, lacked polish or evidence of much research, had left him frustrated and confused about what sense could be made of the experience. "What did you expect—a BBC documentary?" Sheila asked him when he expressed his frustration to his study group. "They're just kids. And it was the first time they'd ever done anything like this before."

Rick's instructor was more direct in his remarks, and suggested that Rick should "stop thinking like a teacher and start thinking like a researcher." The difference, he went on to explain, was that a researcher would not focus on evaluating the quality of the students' academic performance by some pre-established set of criteria, but would instead focus on explaining the dynamics of the situation and its outcomes. Rick was annoyed by the criticism and wondered if the two perspectives could be as neatly separated as was being suggested, but he decided to hold his tongue. To direct his analysis, he returned to the chart outlining his research questions, data sources, and analytical notes, and began to code first his field notes, then the student logs, the first round of interviews (he decided to use the second round to follow up on findings from his initial coding), and then the videos and left-over footage.

No sooner had Rick begun to reread his field notes, however, than the original coding categories of "resistance" and "engagement" seemed somehow not relevant to or expressive of the quality of his students' activities. It was clear that in the first few weeks very little had been accomplished, but it was not so clear that this was because the students were simply messing around or refusing to work. More often, the notes showed it was because of honest mistakes, such as inefficient Internet searches due to misspelled words or because an inappropriate key word had led a student on a wild-goose chase, or because of technical problems or lack of experience with the recording equipment. In other cases, Rick was able to see in retrospect that there were political reasons for some of the problems the students were having. He noted a reference to a conversation in the Girls in War group one day, when an argument ensued over whether to interview Sonia, a student in another class whose brother was also in the armed services, because "Sonia's family are too, you know, military"—implying that was a point of view some in the group did not want in their video. He also noted Curtis's strong defense of the mooning incident and his argument, on principle, to include it in the Support Our Troops video because "it tells it like it is—it's just what we think of them, you know." He had recorded Sanjay's question about whether his father was going to see their video, and began to wonder if this reflected a political concern.

Rick's notes also recorded the three days Tom spent agonizing over the final narrative sentence of his video segment. The video was a very touching tribute to Evan. It consisted of Tom's voice-over narration of photos and scans of newspaper headlines from his football career, juxtaposed against a very gritty montage of photos of the Afghanistan campaign, taken from the Internet. Tom had not given any indication of his brother's or his own position on the war throughout the segment, until the last sentence. In one version, he concluded by saying, "This war has cost some people more than words can express," but decided it was too personal. In another, he said, "This nation is killing its future leaders," but decided it was "too angry" and "people will take it the wrong way." At the end of three days and after close consultation with several other students in the class, Tom finally chose to say, with as little emotion as possible, "No one can ever know how much this war has already cost."

Rick looked through the student logs and transcripts of his first round of interviews, and watched both the video segments and the out takes again, looking for corroborating indicators that it was a range of problems and not "slacking off" that might better account for the slow start of the project. Although the logs were brief and not well-kept and the students were often inarticulate in responding to interview questions, they, too, indicated time lost on searches that went nowhere, problems with using the equipment, and disagreements about how whom to interview and how to frame topics. Against this evidence, Angelina's explanation, "This is harder than it looks. There are a lot of things you have to think about, and something always goes wrong," sounded a good deal more candid and self-aware to Rick than it had before.

Rather than conceptualize students' activities as resistant or engaged, Rick wondered if the master categories of "challenges" and "opportunities" might make more sense. He returned to his field notes and found that he could identify many more incidents in these terms than the original ones. Within the "challenges" category, he identified three types of challenge: academic (reading; conceptualizing problems in academic terms); technical (arising from learning to use equipment and software); and political/representational (deciding what and how to present meanings to an audience). "Opportunities" in his notes seemed to be fewer and narrower. He identified two principal sources of these: models (formats, styles of presentation, and images that were traceable to mass media); and the technology, whose ease of use and formatting was facilitative. In addition, there were a few "key moments"— when an interviewee said something particularly striking or ironic, when "the perfect" photo or audio clip was found, or when the production values of a video clip were particularly crisp—that boosted the students' morale and interest in the project. Rick at first thought of these moments as accidental, but after further review decided that although some seemed serendipitous, others were equally the result of careful planning and perseverance.

In response to the third research question about sources of information the students drew from, Rick made a chart for each video and recorded, scene by scene, what audio, visual, and video images were used, identified the source of each (or made a note to ask in the follow-up interview), and made notes about the style—tempo, length, camera angle, effects—of the scene. His analysis suggested that all the videos drew from the same bank of stylistic tools, which in turn seemed to come largely from music videos and television programs that targeted adolescents, but that the sources of the images themselves were highly differentiated by ethnicity and gender. His field notes and transcripts from the first round of focus interviews corroborated this analysis. In addition, these data sources highlighted the extent to which students from immigrant backgrounds drew from websites and satellite television programs from their home regions.

When Rick turned to his second and fourth research questions about the influence of "ethnicity" on the project, he realized quickly that the simple answer to these questions was that multiple forms of difference obviously figured into the groups the students formed and the topics and tenor of their videos. But he also realized that the groups the students had formed into were not as stereotypical as they first seemed, and that the stances of each video segment were not all as reflective of an obviously identifiable position on the conflict. For example, the Justice for All group consisted of two students of Middle Eastern and two students of Indian descent—groups whose religious differences would seem to have divided them, and the Whose War Is It? group was mixed both by gender and race. The Girls in War group was all female, but racially and ethnically very diverse. They had joined together to provide a "female perspective" on the conflict, but soon became so divided over what that perspective should be that Luis quipped one day that they should rename their group Girls *at* War. The Support Our Troops group consisted of four White males and Peter, an ethnic Chinese second-generation immigrant from Hong Kong. Rick wondered about Peter's affiliation with this group, since the four White males were very working class and "macho" in their demeanor and Peter was something of a "nerd," until he overheard Peter, Jack, and Curtis all discussing their alliance in an online game they logged onto most evenings. Moreover, from what Rick knew of the students' parents' occupations and the students' own career aspirations, social class seemed to have very little to do with the formation of groups.

Rick had assumed that each group had had its own reasons for coming together, until he watched the Support Our Troops group video and then the Whose War Is It? video directly afterward. The former video consisted of a number of interviews with White authority figures in the school and community talking about the potential danger of criticism of the war undermining troop morale and giving "Al Qaeda" an advantage, with patriotic music in the background, while the latter video featured interviews with students and adults in the community who questioned the need for involvement and the impact of the war on families, against a background of hip-hop music and urban images. Watching the two videos in juxtaposition, it seemed to Rick as if they were engaging each other's arguments in debate. Then he watched the "Justice for All" video and saw that it, too, seemed to respond to the arguments of the Support Our Troops video from another angle, as did the Girls in War video, Tom's video, and the Public Opinion video. Could it be, Rick wondered, that although some groups appeared to have organized themselves roughly along personal, gender, or racial/ethnic lines, an equally strong organizing principle within the class was a common antagonism toward the politics and message of the predominantly White male group?

At a meeting later in the week, Rick's presentation of his preliminary findings and their interpretation caught his instructor—now editor—and two of the members of his study group, Chris and Edmund, off guard. "What a change," Chris remarked. "A few weeks ago you were ready to hang this project up and write the kids off as slackers. Now, they're cagey political commentators, struggling to master their craft. Brilliant!" Rick caught the irony in the remark. He quickly qualified his argument, saying that although this looked to be the case, he needed to revisit the data and conduct follow-up interviews to check his interpretations with the students. His instructor agreed, although he also noted that this new interpretation was much more complex theoretically than it had originally seemed. "So, resistance isn't the guideword anymore, eh?" he remarked. "Then, how *would* you theorize what happened in your classroom?"

## Entering the conversation

Beginning researchers, in my experience, are likely to face a number of different challenges when they begin to write with social theory. Reverence for a theoretician or a school of theory, or a lack of clarity about how and the extent to which a theory and one's empirical research project relate, are often very problematic. Equally as challenging is the task of learning about and developing a sense of confidence in the general discourse conventions of research. And finally, there is the issue of which conversation and therefore which set of discourse conventions are appropriate for a particular journal, for a particular research conference, or for a book or book chapter.

The best advice ever given to me about writing academic prose for publication was by Linda Brodkey, who urged her students to imagine that they were "joining a conversation" about a topic that had been going on for some time before they had arrived. Consider the dynamics of this sometimes awkward situation: You've entered a room full of strangers who are arranged at tables more or less according to point of view or historical circumstances, and who are talking among themselves even as they're listening and contributing to a larger conversation within the whole room. Many of them are already accomplished conversationalists, which means they know the history of the issues under discussion, and the points of view, more or less, of nearly everyone in the room, or at least of every table. They know where all the weaknesses of everyone's arguments are (or think they do), and they are practiced in knowing not only what to say but how to say it in order to send a particular message to their audience. Like all language games, there are rules to these conversations, but they can't be gotten in writing; they must be picked up through immersion in the game—the conversation—itself.

From afar, such conversations often appear to be forms of kabuki theatre, ritual set pieces where everyone is playing a role so tightly constricted by tradition that nothing of any significance can ever happen, and the conversation can never progress. But that is not quite the case. The room and the conversation do not exist in a vacuum, but are permeated by social and cultural forces and by other conversations from the outside that are beyond their control, and so their utility, their need to perform some social and cultural function, is always in play. Moreover, many of the participants are quite principled and quite practiced; they are looking for new voices to enter and enliven their discourse. And best of all, most play by rules that are relatively fair.

That is where you come in, especially if you have some new information or a new way of framing an issue or a situation that has grown stale through a lack of fresh perspective. But it won't do, as your intuition probably tells you, to barge into the main conversation on the floor, or even at one of the tables. No, you'll be cut off, or worse. To enter this conversation, you'll need to do something first that may seem very foreign, particularly if you're a graduate student who has focused on the ideas and content of what you've been reading—the *what*—rather than the form in which it is contained—the *how*. You'll need to study the rules of engagement, or the rhetoric, as well as the history of the particular conversation in educational research that you want to enter.

There are two ways to do this. One way is to have a guide—your advisor, perhaps, or someone else who has a proven record of participating in research and theory-based conversations—who will be willing to share with you her knowledge and understanding of the conversation you are interested in entering. By this I do not mean someone who will provide you with a taxonomic outline of all the topics and subtopics covered, but rather someone who will share "war stories" with you of the history of particular conversations, including not only a personalized intellectual history of issues but also, at times, a genealogy of the personalities involved, their alliances and disputes, ideological backgrounds, and so on—the gossip, if you will. As the stories accumulate, the next step is to become familiar with the "classic" texts of these stories, and then to survey the more recent publications that your guide would advise and that you might find using Google Scholar and the resources of a good academic library.

A second, alternative way, if no guide is available, or if you suspect that your guide has strong prejudices that are clouding or otherwise distorting the information being given, or simply if, like me, you are a little hardheaded and determined to find your own way, is to begin by wandering about in the resources of a good academic library, perusing available journals both electronically and in hard copy, and to build a schema, or narrative framework of the conversation about a topic from scratch. This approach is likely to take far more time but it may also yield a sense of the literature and conversation about a topic that is richer and more elaborated than you might otherwise receive. But, beware, also: The impressions you form and the narrative you construct may also be inaccurate in some key ways. It is not always feasible to judge a journal or group of journals by their covers, or even by their contents, without knowing their full history and relations to other journals and their sponsoring organizations. In the end, it is a sound practice to check one's impressions and one's sense of a conversation's history with more experienced others.

The recent publications that you identify in your research are important not only for the information they will provide about the current state of the conversation and debate around issues, but also for the information that can be taken from them about the venues in which discussion is occurring (venues where you might submit your work to enter the conversation). If some of these are journals, you might want to locate hard copies of recent issues and review their contents. Note the general editorial tenor of each journal. Does it include articles and features in which social theory plays a substantial role? What is the style of the writing? Does the journal predominantly feature qualitative or quantitative articles, essays with no original empirical base, or a mixture of all three? What is the tone of these articles? Do authors write in a distanced, "objective" voice, or in a more personal, even confessional or impressionistic voice? How are the articles organized? Are strict conventions for organization (Introduction; Literature Review; Methods; Findings; Discussion; Conclusion) followed, or is there more latitude in the organization of the writing? Some journals in education, such as the Canadian journal, *Curriculum Inquiry*, the Australian journal, *Discourse*, the Anglo-American *Journal of Curriculum Studies*, or the *British Journal of Sociology of Education*, follow a more humanistic rhetorical tradition, in which it is assumed from the overall quality of the paper that data collection procedures were valid and reliable, and require only a brief description. Other journals founded in a more psychologistic, positivistic tradition, such as *Reading Research Quarterly* or the *American Educational Research Journal*, typically insist on a very detailed description of research methods and procedures for both qualitative and quantitative, experimental studies, as an assurance that the data on which claims are based are extensive, coherent, and relatively free from researcher bias.

At this point, it is time to ask some hard, honest questions of your own project. As you conduct this analysis of each journal, ask yourself if your study looks like others in it, in terms of its scope, its design, and in the stance you are taking with regard to the general conversation about the issues you are raising. Is your study one that challenges conventional wisdom and that might conceivably upset someone at the table or perhaps at another table? This is not necessarily a problem, particularly if your evidence is strong and there are others at your table who would be sympathetic to your arguments, but it does mean that you'll need to be particularly careful in how you phrase your argument and attend, a la Toulmin (1958; see Chapter Two) to possible qualifications of your argument and their rebuttal. Or, is your study one that extends ("mops up," after Kuhn [1996]) or adds empirical substantiation to your topic and to the conversation at the table? As you review the rhetorical styles of different journals, you may notice that some editors are more open to and encourage studies that make provocative claims than others, where critique is not as welcome, or where there are a number of "sacred cows"—topics or schools of theory that are not open to challenge. (For example, in many US journals, John Dewey is a revered figure whose work is open to discussion and interpretation, but only along some very standard lines of argument, and never to direct criticism.) A last but very important question to ask is whether you can see yourself organizing your study and writing in a style that complements a particular journal's practices. If you can't, or if you can only see yourself trying to mimic or parody its style rather than write honestly in its manner, then that journal—that table and conversation—may not be for you.

Entering a particular conversation in educational research becomes even more complicated when a study makes extensive use of a social theoretical framework. In the analysis of each journal or book in a series, it is important to pay close attention, first, to whether social theory appears regularly in its articles, and then, to which theorists or schools of theory are referenced, which are not, and what stance is typically taken toward the theory, i.e. are theories accepted more or less as valid, or are they the object of critique and qualification? The editors and reviewers of some journals may harbor a preference for some schools of theory, such as social constructivism, but hold others in disdain, such as poststructuralism or the work of particular theorists such as Michel Foucault or Pierre Bourdieu. Be wary also of journals or series that may specialize in publishing studies grounded in a particular school of theory or theorist, or that have a strong political (leftist or rightist) agenda. Many times the conversation in these journals is very tightly developed around a particular reading, or interpretation, of a body of work. The politics of these journals can often result in a treacherous exercise in which your interpretation and application of your theoretical framework will be scrutinized against the journal's, and will typically be found wanting. Sometimes these prejudices are not immediately apparent; in that case, it helps to check your impressions against the advice of someone with a history of participation in a particular journal's conversations.

Some final qualification of the argument that it is important to know exactly which conversation one wants to enter and what its history and rules are *before* one begins to write may be in order here. There is a school of thought in composition studies, best articulated by the expressivist camp (e.g. Elbow 1973), that a preoccupation with the conventions of a particular genre or style of writing will likely result either in writer's block or in writing that is formulaic and dull, and that captures little of the writer's own voice or the originality of the material. From this perspective, it would be far more advisable for researchers to allow their data and their own narrative and expository inclinations to guide the organizational and stylistic decisions made as a research study is written up, and then to match the resulting text with a suitable outlet for publication.

I disagree with this perspective for a number of reasons. First, as I have argued elsewhere (Dressman 1993), when novice writers take or are given free reign over the parameters of their writing, the results are typically not works of great originality and voice, but texts lacking in coherence and audience awareness. It is important when learning how to write (and experienced writers often ask) to have models so that their rules of play can be studied as one writes, not so that they can be formulaically memorized and parodied. Second, in my experience as a reviewer and editor, I have noted how many manuscripts are rejected, not because they do not have a potential contribution to make to the field of education, but because their authors have not made the effort to join any particular conversation, or because the audience they have in mind is not the audience for that journal. Accomplished researchers seldom begin to write up their research without having a very clear idea of where they will submit their manuscript; indeed, many researchers, including myself, begin to plan their writing for particular journals or other publication venues (books or chapters) very early in the research process, sometimes even before they have begun to collect their data. And third, the suggestion that the written discourses of educational research are so oppressive in their conventions that they effectively squelch the voices and ideas of new scholars is specious, in my opinion. The goal of writing educational research for publication is not to "express yourself," it is to contribute to the development of shared knowledge. There are many different conversations going on within educational research simultaneously, and many different tables to join. If one table does not suit your study, your perspective, or your temperament, find another one that does. But by all means, do not remain a lone voice or become little more than a heckler, outside the bounds of any conversation, because from either of these positions, your contribution to the field is likely never to be taken seriously.

Rick's concluding interviews, conducted during the summer at local coffee shops and eateries where the students were more relaxed than in school, corroborated his working theory that the difficulties the students had in producing their video segments were more likely due to a combination of academic, technical, and political challenges than to resistance to the assignment or to school itself. Sanjay reported that he was worried his father would think their video was "too radical" and would "make trouble." Jack reviewed the problems he faced doing online research, admitting that he'd "never done anything like that before; you know, I'm used to letting other students do that part." And Angelina recounted the frustration she faced with "getting the sound and the picture right" during shooting and losing or mislabeling video tapes and "having to go back and shoot some scenes over and over again." Even Curtis was forthcoming about the mooning incident. He admitted, "Yeah, we did it for laughs. But it was also, you know, our opinion. It was serious, too, you know."

With his data coded and with responses to each of his research questions formulated and substantiated by his coding results, Rick turned to the manuscript for the book chapter he'd been asked to write. He'd met with his course instructor, now editor, and discussed the editor's expectations for the chapter. "You've got some solid data that raises questions about two theoretical arguments," the instructor told him.

"I'd advise you to raise these two arguments briefly in your introduction, then even more briefly describe the video project and suggest the questions it raises for these theories. In the literature review that follows, provide a short but more elaborated discussion of social and cultural production and of the recent literature on multiliteracies."

He explained that the purpose of the literature review was

"to set the reader up—to frame the theoretical implications and significance of your findings in advance, so that as they read your account and analysis of the project, they'll have your reading of the literature on students' resistance and multiliteracies in mind. Then, in your discussion section, you can return to the issues of the literature review and discuss your findings' implications for these two theories."

"And in the conclusion?" Rick asked.

"Focus on the practical implications of your findings for teaching modern history. From your presentation, it seemed like the students were more engaged than they had been before the project, but you also suggested that most of the learning they did was about video production, not about the conflict. Is that right?"

Rick nodded. "So, if you were going to do this again, what might you do differently? Speculate, but ground your ideas in your data and your experience as a teacher."

The length of the manuscript was to be no more than 35 pages. "If you were writing a manuscript for submission to a journal, you'd probably need to write a lengthy description of your methods, to demonstrate that your data is reliable and valid. But people read book chapters differently; they want to focus on ideas and issues, and will assume that your research was carefully designed and collected. So, describe the setting, the participants, and the length of the project, and list what data you collected and how you analyzed it in a page or two." He gave Rick two photocopies of recently published similar book chapters, to use as models, and they arranged to meet in two weeks to discuss Rick's writing progess.

Rick had always believed himself to be a very capable and fluent writer, able to grasp the conventions of a new genre quickly and use them to express himself and his ideas clearly, and so he was surprised at how difficult it was to write an introduction to his study. In his first draft, he decided he would begin by introducing himself and the context of the study, and then explain how his reading for two courses had led to a research project that explored the use of video and its effects on student engagement and learning. Three pages into the draft, he realized that he had not yet begun to describe the project or its theoretical framework. *Too detailed and too chatty*, he thought, and tried to edit the three pages down; but even condensed to two pages, he realized that his readers' attention would soon be wandering. Beginning again, he thought this time that he would focus first on theory, in language suggesting his seriousness as a scholar. But again, after three pages he stopped. *Too pompous*, he thought; *this doesn't sound like me*. After a week of struggle, he shared his frustration with Gwen. She asked him what the main idea or problem of the chapter was.

"What got me started was that the studies of secondary students' behavior that we read in the first course did not suggest that there was anything teachers could do about their students' resistance to schooling. The readings for the second course described adolescents' engagement with electronic media, but they also suggested schools were dead zones. Then, when Tom's brother died I had the idea to use video to see if it would engage my third period class's interest, and it did, but not with complete success."

Having to explain the issues verbally to someone else seemed to bring the topic into focus and order for Rick. The next day, he composed this opening sentence: "Neither 30 years of research into the culture of secondary schools nor more recent research and theory about adolescents' use of electronic media offers much direction or hope for practicing secondary teachers." He followed this with a second sentence, in which he cited ethnographic studies from his Secondary Schooling in Social Context course and characterized their implications for teachers as suggesting "that secondary schools are typically places where students are preoccupied with developing social and cultural identities and practices, sometimes to the exclusion of learning academic content knowledge." His third sentence cited references about electronic communications from his Youth Cultures course, and characterized these as suggesting "that in an age of global communications and electronically mediated texts, youth need the knowledge and skills that teachers and schools are supposed to offer even less."

Rick was tempted to continue with an elaborated discussion of theory and research, but decided to wait until the next section of the manuscript. In his second paragraph, he related the arguments of his first paragraph to his own experience, admitting, "As a teacher of modern history in a secondary school on the edge of a major city, many of the claims made in this research and theory do seem to ring true." Without describing specific instances, in two sentences he described his students' apparent lack of interest in his curriculum, his attempts to address this problem, and his continuing frustration with his students' academic responses. He concluded the paragraph by noting that his reading for two courses had helped to provide an analysis of the problem, but posed no practical response.

In his third paragraph, Rick introduced his research project. He mentioned Evan's death and described it as a "catalyzing moment" that prompted him to turn to video as an "electronically mediated response to a social and curricular crisis" in his school, and that, as a research project, he hoped would help answer four research questions, which he listed (see Table 3.1). In a fourth, short paragraph, he foreshadowed the complexity of the outcome by noting that the findings of the study "suggest a more complicated but still hopeful role for electronically mediated curricula than I could have ever anticipated."

Rick e-mailed a draft of the introduction to his editor, who replied that he was off to a good start, and should follow up in the next section with a more detailed discussion of the theoretical issues he'd raised and the studies that backed his argument. Emboldened, Rick gathered his readings for the courses, tracked down some of the references from these readings, and began to write the next section of the chapter, which he titled "Theory and Related Research." He was surprised at how much there was to write about. He decided to provide a chronological overview of the history of the literature on social and cultural production and reproduction. In two pages, he wrote a concise explanation of the Marxist perspective that supported much of the research, and then provided summaries of a page or so of six seminal studies, beginning with Willis (1977) and continuing through an edited volume by Dolby and Dimitriadis (2004) that reviewed and updated discussions and research grounded in Willis's work. Then he turned to the literature on electronic media and youth culture, reviewing the claims of multiple articles and edited books that the school curriculum had been left behind in these new times, but that it could possibly "catch up" if these technologies and the new pedagogies they facilitated were massively embraced.

However, when Rick shared the introduction and seventeen pages of literature review he'd completed with his study group, their response was not what he expected. "I liked the introduction," Sheila told him. "But I got lost and started wondering, 'What's the point?' after five pages of the next section." Chris and Edmund agreed. "It's important stuff," Chris said. "But I already knew about most of this. I wanted to read about how it related to your research, but you barely mentioned that."

Rick was dismayed and later shared the group's feedback with his editor, who admitted he had to agree with them. "I think the problem is that your readers already knew about much of what you wrote," he said. "You might assume that other readers will, too, or that they are reading your chapter not to learn about these topics, but to read about what's new, your study, and how your research relates to your theoretical framework." His advice was to "stick close to the two problems you identified in your introduction— the lack of concern for learning academic content that you saw in the earlier literature, and whether and how electronic media can address the resistance that is described in the literature and that you experienced in your class."

He urged Rick to "take a few days off, then go through your review with a pencil and cut out anything that doesn't directly contribute to supporting the two points you're making. And look," he concluded, "Right now you're already on page 19 of this manuscript and you haven't even gotten to your methods, your findings, or your discussion and conclusion. So, you need to cut way back and get this review in proportion. Remember, you'll get a chance to return to this literature and discuss some of it in greater depth in the later sections of the chapter."

Rick allowed this feedback to settle in over the weekend. On Monday, he sat down and in grim determination began to cut all his lengthy descriptions of research, along with his discussions of the issues each study raised and his opinion of them. He retained the studies themselves, but instead of writing about each, used topic sentences to group them and then cited them as references, with occasional short discussions of how these studies contributed to his two principal arguments. In two days, he'd pared the length of the section to six pages. He moved on to a section he titled, "Designing the Study," and wrote a three-paragraph description of the setting, including a two-sentence account of Evan's death and its impact, described the diversity of his students, their lack of engagement in the class, and the video assignment. With reference to his research questions, he listed the data he collected and his plan for analysis. In meetings with his study group and editor two weeks later, their consensus was that the chapter was "shaping up." At last, Rick thought; *now, for the interesting part of the chapter!*

## Findings, discussions, and conclusions

The decisions that authors make about the tone, point of view, and organization of sections that present research findings and their implications largely depend on the interplay of three factors: the venue and audience an author is writing for; the scope and type of the research project and its data; and the perspective, or stance, an author wants readers to take toward her or his findings. Historically, the conventions of educational research have evolved from the fields of psychology and sociology/anthropology. In their formative years early in the last century, both these disciplines stressed the scientific, objective nature of their endeavors. True to the logic and practices of modernism, they operated from the perspective that an objectifiable social reality existed, whose organization and dynamics could be discovered through rational processes that absented the researcher and his or her prejudices from their explication. In keeping with this belief, the writing up of research was to be performed much as one would write a scientific lab report, stating "the facts" as plainly, objectively, and comprehensively as possible (so that other researchers might replicate the study, to demonstrate its validity). Any involvement of the researcher in the research process itself would need to be reported, but only as a *limitation* that qualified claims of generalizability and replicability.

In the last quarter of the twentieth century, however, these conventions became the object of withering critique, particularly from within the fields of sociology and anthropology, so much so that a schism developed and remains to this day in educational research between *quantitative* research practices, which have retained their faith in the possibility of objective knowledge, or truth, and so in their writing practices as well, and *qualitative* research practices, which have increasingly not only acknowledged but embraced the particularity of research contexts and the involvement of the researcher and her or his point of view in the writing up of findings. A full discussion of the variety of approaches to writing qualitative and ethnographic research is beyond the scope of this chapter (see Kamberelis and Dimitriadis 2005; Goodall 2000; Clifford and Marcus 1986; and Atkinson *et al.* 2003, for several book-length discussions of these issues). One of the most useful and clearest taxonomies of qualitative writing was proposed by Van Maanen (1988), who described three general narrative approaches: the realist, the impressionist, and the confessional. Realist approaches are written principally in the third-person, and in keeping with the objectivist tradition out of which educational research developed, they aim to provide readers with an emotionally unadorned, almost "photographic" image and impression of the events and patterns described. Impressionist approaches are often written in the first-person, and aim to create, as would an impressionist painting, a sense of immediate emotional and aesthetic involvement on the part of readers—to immerse them in the context of a setting and produce meanings and understandings that are highly personalized and almost visceral, as opposed to coolly rational and detached. The writing is typically experimental, ranging in format from novelistic, stream-of-consciousness to poetry to forms of dramatic live or video performance. Confessional approaches place the experience of the researcher at the center of the narrative. They are highly subjective in focus, and typically involve some admission on the part of the researcher of a level of involvement that has transgressed the boundaries of academic (and sometimes social and cultural) propriety. These narratives are typically written by seasoned researchers for other researchers, and are meant to challenge, or interrupt, the conventions and unacknowledged biases within a field or area of discussion.

However, despite more than 20 years of critique and experimentation, the normative approach to qualitative writing in educational research remains a modified form of realism, in which impressionistic and confessional styles of writing are interspersed within accounts intended to be read as accurate, if not fully objective, representations of actual people and events. With a few notable exceptions, such as the journals *Qualitative Inquiry, International Journal of Qualitative Studies in Education* (QSE), or *Taboo*, and some edited collections in books whose express purpose is to push the stylistic edges of qualitative writing, most educational research journals publish fully impressionistic or confessional studies infrequently, and then often with a wink to readers that this is an "experimental" piece of writing.

Within a modified realist approach, how findings are presented varies broadly, depending upon the type of data collected. When the chronology of events is important—when a situation develops through a sequence of events, or there is a comparison to be made before and after some point in time—the presentation of findings typically begins with the narration of that chronology, followed by subsections that focus on specific patterns or events within the chronology. Reports of interview data may begin with broad findings, and then proceed to the presentation of specific or lesser patterns, or to exceptional cases. Presentation of multiple case studies typically begins with individual cases or cases grouped in juxtaposition to each other, followed by the presentation of patterns across cases or the contrast of patterns found with one group or individual with others. As a general heuristic or rule of thumb, then, the presentation of findings in a modified realist approach begins in broad or general terms, followed by subsections that focus on specific findings or featured points of analysis.

The integration of social theory within the presentation of findings also varies, depending on the extent to which the author has relied on theory to warrant different arguments within a study. In my analysis of 69 literacy research studies that made use of social theory (Dressman 2007), I found four patterns of theory use. In the least integrated use of social theory, authors described the relevance of a social theory to their study in the introductory or literature review sections of their studies but did not refer back to their theoretical framework in their presentation of findings, their discussions, or their conclusions. In these cases, social theory typically warranted the premise of the study, or served as a *foundational platform*, but did not contribute in any significant way to the design of the study, the analysis of data, or the presentation and interpretation of findings.

In a second pattern, I termed researchers' use of social theory a *focal apparatus*, or lens. In these studies, social theory was discussed in the introduction and literature reviews and in the discussion and concluding sections of a study, but was not referenced in the methods or findings (the middle) sections. I speculated that in many instances this pattern probably occurred either because the authors wanted to convey that their data collection and analysis had been "unbiased" by a theoretical framework, or because social theory had been applied to the analysis of findings after a study had been designed and data had been collected and analyzed, almost as an afterthought. In these studies, authors seemed to use social theory as a lens, or reflective device for speculating about the implications of findings, rather than more declaratively, as the warrant for making claims with a degree of certainty.

The third and fourth patterns of theory use that were identified made use of social theory in a far more complex and integrated way. Many researchers made use of social theory as a narrative, or *dialogical scaffold*, that is, as a framework that overtly structured nearly every section and decision made in the research process, from the conceptualization of a study to the design of data collection and analytic practices, to the interpretation of findings and the discussion of implications. Very often, the central focus of these studies seemed to be the promulgation of the theoretical framework rather than its application as a tool for making sense of experience—that is, findings often served to illustrate a theoretical perspective. Moreover, the authors of studies using theory as a dialogical scaffold rarely qualified their claims about social theory, or offered any explanation of how theories originating in the analysis of distant events or time periods could so unproblematically be applied to the analysis of local situations in the present. From a Toulminian (Toulmin 1958) perspective, these practices often resulted in arguments lacking qualification or rebuttal, and in which distinctions among evidence, warrant, and backing were blurred. As a consequence, studies using this pattern often presented original and even poetic interpretations of situations, but interpretations that also sometimes seemed contrived and open to challenge on multiple grounds. In the fourth pattern that was identified, social theory functioned as a *dialectical scaffold*—a framework that was itself somewhat modified and refined through its encounter with the experience of the research. In these studies, which were also among the fewest in number of the 69 articles analyzed, the use of social theory was nearly as extensive within a study as in the dialogical scaffold pattern, but the application of theory to the analysis of the data was qualified and rebutted by the researcher. The result was a tension in the study between the social theory used and the experience of the research—a testing of both findings and theory, that resulted in a finer-grained and more complicated analysis and presentation of findings than in the three other patterns. In some cases, a single theory was challenged by evidence from a study; in others, evidence was used to evaluate the utility of two opposing theoretical perspectives. In all cases, from a Toulminian perspective, the arguments made were the most fully elaborated and developed, and included all the elements of argumentation identified by Toulmin—data (evidence), a clearly explicated warrant, backing, and qualification and rebuttal of claims.

Ironically, although studies that use social theory as a dialectical scaffold also make the most complex use of theory, they are also frequently the least conclusive and self-contained in their concluding discussions and implications. Instead, studies such as these tend to call for further explication of theoretical concepts and their application to the description and analysis of social phenomena, as well as for further empirical research. In so doing, they also open connections to future and current research that makes use of related theoretical frames—to practices of comparison and contrast that in time may shape the development of more rigorous, skeptical, interrelated, and ultimately more valid bodies of general knowledge about a phenomenon.

Rick thought he knew exactly how to present his findings. His plans were confirmed in his next meeting with his editor, who urged him to "lead with the evidence, followed by a discussion of how it relates to your theoretical framework. But then, point to evidence that does not fit with theory, and suggest alternative explanations. In your discussion and conclusion, you can talk about the implications of what you found and outline possible future projects."

Rick also wondered about how and where to talk about his own experience, since he was both a participant and the researcher. He decided that he did not want to "play God" in the text, writing omnisciently in third person. His feelings and attitudes during the project were important, but they would not be at the center of the analysis; that was reserved for the students and their videos.

He began to write:

> After five years of teaching modern history, I had worked through the challenges of classroom management and lesson planning and was regarded as a successful teacher. However, it was the rare occasion when my students showed more than a minimal interest in course topics or assignments.

Rick then described several examples from assignments and student comments to illustrate his point, including an anecdote in which he shared his frustration with colleagues in the teachers' workroom one day, only to find that everyone else was having the same experience as him, except they didn't find it as objectionable.

> This image of schooling as an almost autonomic process in which teachers and students are paradoxically both acquiescent and resourceful in playing roles that lead to seemingly predictable consequences would seem congruent with the image of schooling depicted in the literature on social and cultural production and reproduction,

Rick wrote in his next paragraph, followed by illustrative parallel examples from his experiences and that body of social theory. "What may be a new twist, however," he wrote in a subsequent paragraph, "Is the extent to which students' lives, and consequently the strategies of resistance and cultural and social reproduction available to them, are mediated by their ubiquitous connection to, and use of, electronic media and communications." As evidence of this claim, he then presented the findings from his survey and observations of students' uses of cell phones, instant messaging, satellite television, and other media in his classroom and in their daily lives.

In the next subsection, titled "Reproduction and Video Production," Rick told the story, supported largely by evidence from his field notes, of the making of the video and that concluded with an analysis of the students' final products. "Evan's tragic death served as the catalyst for an experiment 'testing' whether the introduction of electronic technologies and multiple literacies would produce a higher degree and quality of engagement with schooling than had previously been the case," he wrote in his first paragraph. He described the formation of student groups and themes of the videos, to be organized under the general topic of "The War at Home," and included a table that provided information about the gender, ethnicity, religious backgrounds, citizenship and status, and parents' occupations, as an indicator of social class. He did not discuss the anomalies in grouping that he had noticed, deciding to present this analysis and its implications in his discussion section.

Rick provided a brief synopsis of the sequence of events during the shooting and editing phases of the project without discussing his coding of these as evidence of challenges and opportunities (as opposed to evidence of resistance or engagement). He recounted his own frustration during this period, followed by the changes that took place in the students' apparent enthusiasm once they began to edit and add titles, soundtracks, and narration to their video texts. When he came to presenting a description of each group's video, however, he balked. First, he thought he would present a summary of the content, style, and message of each video and follow these with a cross-comparative analysis. But after taking three pages to write the summary of one group's video, he realized that this subsection of his findings could run to 20 or more pages, and would include so much information that readers would likely become confused. Starting again, he took a week to do "what I should have done in the first place," he later told Edmund and Chris— inventory and code each shot in each video for its length, stylistic features, and origin of content (websites, interviews, other media). He compiled this information for each video in chart format, along with a one-sentence synopsis of the intended message of each, which he had thought to verify with each group during their final interviews. He then wrote a two-page overview of these findings, making repeated reference to information in the table.

Rick's editor and his study group were pleased with Rick's presentation of findings, which totaled 12 pages. "I get a very clear idea of what happened during the project, what the issues were and how they were resolved, and what the final videos looked like," Rick's editor told him.

"Yeah, the only question's now, what does it all mean?!" Chris laughed.

Indeed. Rick knew that he'd been deliberately "holding back" on the latter, more theoretical parts of his analysis until the discussion. But how could he present these in a manner that made them seem to flow logically from his narrative? And, there were some issues he hadn't yet accounted for theoretically, particularly the composition of the groups, and the fact that social class did not seem to be as determining in his narrative and analysis as it was in the theoretical and research literature he'd been referencing. Later at the pub he told Edmund that when he tried to write, he couldn't decide what to say first.

He was reminded, in the end, of his initial research questions, and, as mechanical and inelegant as it seemed, after some thought he realized his discussion of the remaining issues could be coherently organized as a series of responses to these. After a brief introduction in which he summarized his findings, Rick opened his discussion section by returning to his first research question about the efficacy of new technologies in engaging his students' academic interest. He noted that the response to this question was more mixed and complex than he originally anticipated. Rick's coding of field notes and interviews indicated that the pattern of apparent resistance to the assignment that frustrated him in the initial weeks of the project was more likely due to three challenges inherent in the task itself, rather than to the forms of political and economic resistance to the process of schooling that had been identified and described previous research and theory. He proceeded to name the three challenges he had identified, and to provide examples from his data to illustrate the academic challenges some of his students, particularly those with a history of problems with reading, had faced, such as initial problems with learning to shoot video with proper lighting and sound, and challenges the groups faced in deciding among themselves what their message would be and how it would most effectively be conveyed.

In his illustration of his last point, Rick drew from student interviews and his inventory of the video segments, as well as from the students' out takes, which showed that not only Tom but several other groups had tried and ultimately abandoned multiple phrasings in their attempts to craft a precise political statement for a presumed audience of parents and community member. The increase in productivity toward the end could similarly be attributed to two "opportunities" in the form of accessible models from the mass media whose appropriated formats were apparent across each video, and in the user friendly format of the editing software, which quickly lent a slick and "professional" look to the students' video clips, and resulted in a boost to their confidence and sense of purpose. Clearly, then, most of the students were not resisting the assignment at all, but were, in fact, struggling to execute it in as meaningful a way as possible.

However, he also argued that it was not clear to what extent the students' engagement was due to the novelty of the technology or to the timeliness of the topic and the emotions generated by Evan's death. He wrote:

> What will happen once the use of video production becomes routine, or when it is used to teach about topics that are an important but less immediately relevant part of the curriculum, or when there is no catalyzing moment to fire students' emotions?

He concluded:

> This project has demonstrated that the use of new technologies can interrupt typical processes of cultural and social reproduction in schools. However, much more research using video as a teaching medium in routine contexts needs to be done before it can be claimed that it is the technologies themselves and not their novelty or a novel situation that engages students' interests.

Rick then responded to his third research question, which asked about the content of the video segments. He documented the resourcefulness of the students in drawing stylistically from music videos and television programs popular with youth in the production of their videos. Yet, he also noted that from a history teacher's perspective, the project could not be considered a complete success, nor could it fully serve as a model for assignments on other topics. As evidence in support of these claims, Rick noted how little information that could be traced to research appeared in each video. His field notes, the students' logs, and the videos themselves indicated that the only significant use of the Internet or other media for information was by the members of the Justice for All group, who relied heavily on information and photographs from foreign websites such as the Arab news network Al Jazeera in their presentation of alternative views of the conflict in Afghanistan and the Middle East. It was not clear or obvious, he noted, how much new information the students had learned about the conflict, or even how much they'd learned or come to respect each other's points of views.

In his response to the second and fourth research questions, about the influence of students' social and cultural backgrounds on their project decisions and final video segments, Rick presented evidence from his analysis of the student groups to argue that except for the three working-class boys who joined to form the Support Our Troops group, social class did not seem to be as determining a factor as ethnicity, religion, and gender, but that other factors, such as associations formed online and political interests that cut across lines of gender and ethnicity, also influenced how the students grouped themselves. In addition, he provided evidence from the analysis of the individual video segments to suggest that students also grouped themselves and seemed to compose their videos in opposition to the pro-military, pro-government position taken by the Support Our Troops group in their video. Rick concluded that because social class and economics could not be shown to have motivated the formation of most student groups or their response to the assignment, the narratives of social and cultural production and reproduction theory did not seem to account, in large part, for the findings presented here.

But if that was the case, he admitted to Chris, Edmund, and Sheila one evening at the pub, he was "stumped," and wondered what theoretical explanation there might be for his findings, "or if they were even worth theorizing about."

"Well, there are patterns here, I think, that need explanation," said Edmund. "And you know, I've been thinking about your class and how different it was from the students in those earlier studies and how different the world is from just 15 years ago. It used to be that you'd have one, two ethnic groups in a school, maybe, and everyone was pretty much in the same social class. But now—how many immigrants or children of immigrants do you have? How many different countries? And how many of them stay in touch with those countries regularly, even go back to visit?"

"A lot," Rick said. "But they aren't grouping exactly by ethnicity, either. So, what's your point?"

"But maybe they are," Sheila suggested. "Like you said, it seemed as though the students grouped themselves to make different points in opposition to the White males—and Peter—in your class. So, maybe there are two ethnic groups in your class, Them—those White boys—and Not Them—everybody else. And you see the immigrant kids getting together in groups and the girls getting together, and then there are the students who are sort of out of it, you know, on the fringes so far of a massive shift in social alignments, the ones you placed in the Public Opinion and Student Perspectives groups."

"That's a theory?!" Rick laughed.

"Actually," Edmund said, "It sounds a lot like what I've been reading about in my summer course on globalization. There's a book you should take a look at, *Modernity at Large*, by Arjun Appadurai. He writes about shifting categories of identity, how people form themselves globally into nations that no longer, if they ever did, conform to the geographic boundaries of states, how it's imagination, media, and travel and technologies that unites people these days. Maybe your students are doing something like what Appadurai suggests."

Rick was skeptical, but thought this new theory was worth at least reading about. He borrowed Edmund's book (Appadurai 1996) and over the next few days skipped around in its chapters. As Edmund had described, Appadurai described a world in which technological advances had produced a number of "scapes," or global cultural flows—*ethnoscapes, mediascapes, technoscapes, financescapes, and ideoscapes* (p. 33)—which challenged former "master narratives," or ways of making sense of human culture (p. 52), and had led to the "deterritorialization" of social and cultural identity (p. 53). In this new global order, images and ideas circulated freely from West to East and North to South and back, providing people in formerly distant corners of the world with access to a wider range of possible lives and lifestyles, or social imaginaries, than ever before. Advances in travel and communications also enabled people to associate more easily with others in distant parts of the world, and to form affinity groups and identities determined not by physical geography or tradition, but by taste, religion, and personal desire, and in opposition to other groups that would deny or otherwise obstruct their imagination's fulfillment.

As Rick read, he could see some parallels between the circulation of ideas and groupings in his class's video project and Appadurai's description of the dynamics of the global cultural order, but he also noted that Appadurai's theorizing had a very dark side to it, and that was its explanation for how the frustration of social imaginations accounted for the rise of terrorist groups and the disintegration of states that had been relatively stable. And, he wondered how Appadurai would explain the recent round of terrorist bombings in London, which were organized and carried out by a group of physicians of cross-national order, that is, people who had risen to the highest strata of the professional world, and whose own social imaginaries would seem to have been fulfilled. These weren't the down-and-out desperate types that he assumed formed the ranks of terrorist groups; in education, culture, and social standing they were more like, well, like him.

But then Rick remembered the racist incident that had startled him at the beginning of his career, and the even more casually racist way he'd found acceptance by his students as "Spanish," rather than Latino. He remembered how chillingly "other" he'd felt for a long time towards the very people whom he was professionally committed to serving. And then he wondered what it would be like to be a physician, in intense personal but usually only fleeting contact with patients and perhaps even colleagues from another culture, people who never really got to know you as a person, and who again and again said things to you that were casually racist. He thought about how tempting it might be, after many, many such incidents, to want to send them a message that couldn't and wouldn't be ignored, to teach them—not them personally, but their culture—a lesson.

In the end, Rick decided that he did not have the evidence to support this theoretical analysis fully, although it seemed intuitively correct to him. He hadn't discussed Appadurai's work in his introductory literature review or used it to inform his research questions or coding, and so it seemed to him that he could not make more than a tentative use of it in his discussion of his findings. Moreover, he had not read enough of Appadurai's work or its commentaries to understand its implications fully himself. In the final subsection of his discussion, he noted that the groups his students formed and the content of their videos could not be explained by his original theoretical framework. He suggested that Appadurai's theory of globalization's effects on social and cultural identity provided one possible account of how and why his students grouped themselves as they did, and he drew illustrative parallels for readers between his evidence and Appadurai's work.

In the concluding section of the chapter, Rick restated his findings in summary form, and called for three issues that needed further attention. One of these was for the study of video production as an educational tool in more routine, less emotionally charged, contexts. A second was for the study of how students from a diverse range of backgrounds developed cultural and social identities within a new technological order. And a third, contingent on findings from the second indicating that Appadurai's theory or something similar to it was accurate in its account of shifting social and cultural alignments, was a call for a new approach to teaching history and social education—one built not on the transmission of fixed narratives of history and society, but one focused more on promoting dialogue and exchange among all the social imaginaries operating within a single classroom, school, or community.

Rick submitted his completed manuscript to his former instructor, now editor, who was pleased with its structure and conclusions, and he shared copies with Chris, Sheila, and Edmund, who were also congratulatory. Rick was proud of the study and its analysis, but he also knew how tentative his findings and conclusions were, and how much future research and refinement of his ideas remained to be done. "Who knows if I got any of it right, really," he told them modestly.

## Summary and conclusion

This chapter took up the proposition that the writing of educational research is a rhetorical activity in which the process of composing a written presentation of findings—the making of an argument designed to persuade knowledgeable others of its validity—is also the process whereby researchers construct new knowledge in a manner that its relevance to broader, more general bodies of knowledge can be shared with others. Within this process, social theory functions as a schema, or framework—a symbolic apparatus whereby the general meaning of data collected in local contexts and its relation to other studies sharing a similar theoretical framework can be examined. However, I also argued in this chapter that this process is most valid and effective in cases where the researcher approaches both her or his framework and data critically, asking difficult questions about the relevance and distance of theoretical concepts from the empirical evidence to which they are applied, and seeking constantly to identify not only where and how data and theory are congruent, but where and how they are incongruent as well. Finally and most pragmatically, the politics of finding a publishing outlet, or venue, that is a good fit for one's project and the importance of learning the history and conversational rules of its discourses were discussed.

Because he was offered the chance to publish his study as a chapter in an edited volume and was able to work closely with an editor from the start, Rick Chavez's entrance into the conversations of educational research was made easier than it is for many first-time authors. However, Rick was still held, and held himself, to the conventions of modified realism, organizationally and stylistically, in his composing process, which included a strict page limit that in the end actually helped his writing and arguments to remain focused and clear. Moreover, Rick remained highly skeptical and conservative in his representation of the implications of his findings and their congruence with his original theoretical frame. His composing process and reflexive stance toward social and cultural production and reproduction theory were characteristic of studies in which social theory functioned as a "dialectical scaffold" (Dressman 2007). In keeping with this stance, even when he discovered an alternate theoretical framework late in his analysis that seemed to offer a parsimonious account of how and why his students grouped themselves as they did and produced videos that were oppositional to the politics of one group in the class, he remained circumspect in his endorsement of the alternate theory, and called instead for further research that would investigate its general validity.

In conclusion, I must note that the arguments and illustrations offered in this chapter for research as a rhetorical process, and for the critical use of social theory as a means to find the general meaning and implications within qualitative and ethnographic studies, do not represent conventional wisdom or practice within educational research as a whole. In the United States, at least, despite a clear trend over the last quarter century away from large-scale experimental and quantitative research and toward smaller-scale qualitative studies conducted in a variety of local settings, the use of social theory as a framework for the doing of research is still typically regarded as suspect—a gimmick borrowed from the humanities that dilutes (or even pollutes) the usefulness of social scientific knowledge and its implications for the making of educational and social policy. It is to an examination of this situation, and to a final argument for the utility of social theory, when applied across multiple studies in a manner that is critically reflexive, that I turn in the next and concluding chapter.

# Chapter 5

# Social theory and the production of general educational knowledge

## Binaries of educational research

The principal focus of this book in its Introduction and preceding chapters has been on the use of social theory *within* individual research projects—on their value as sources of alternative perspectives; on an overview of the multiple perspectives they provide; on the interpretive and rhetorical condition of research and its implications for the use of social theory; and, interwoven with the narrative of one fictional teacher's project, on the practical challenges and opportunities of using social theory as a framework for educational research. In this concluding chapter, I turn to an examination of social theory's potential use in bringing a large number of currently disparate studies based on data collected in seemingly unrelated localities by individual researchers into greater relation with each other, and so into greater discursive coherence as a body of general, practical knowledge about educational phenomena.

This is a daunting task, not so much because of the intellectual and theoretical challenges it raises, but because it flies in the face of the history and of much that is written and taught in graduate courses today about social theory and qualitative and ethnographic research. Historically, social theories' prospective roles in the production of general educational knowledge are bound up in the discourses of multiple binaries, or naturalized oppositions, that have largely governed the politics of social science and educational research over the last four decades. With respect to the social sciences, from their beginnings in the 1890s to the 1960s, qualitative ethnographic and quantitative research methods were largely viewed as complementary paths to the development of knowledge that was assumed to be relatively objective in its representation of human social behavior. According to Atkinson *et al.* (2003), researchers during this period were aware of and concerned about their own and others' possible biases in the design and interpretation of research and attempted to compensate for these, even if they typically maintained their rhetorical claims to objectivity in their writing.

In sociology, although Durkheim and Weber advocated and employed different uses of research (Durkheim favored statistical and experimental studies; Weber took a more global and qualitative but equally large-scale approach), each viewed their work as contributing to the understanding of an objective social reality. Later, from the 1930s through the 1960s, researchers in the Chicago School of Sociology conducted studies of multiple social problems that were primarily ethnographic and local in their data sources, and which were used to propose general theories of social behavior. In anthropology, early researchers such as Franz Boaz, Ruth Benedict, and Bronislaw Malinowski undertook studies of "vanishing primitive cultures" modeled after practices of natural history used by nineteenth century researchers such as Charles Darwin. They cataloged artifacts, mapped villages, analyzed the structure of languages, recorded (and participated in) cultural practices and even measured the skulls and bodies of "primitives," who had been romanticized in travel literature and in the writings of early European armchair philosophers (e.g. Rousseau) as more noble and purer versions of "civilized" people like themselves—even as their governments and fellow citizens exploited their bodies, their natural resources, and perhaps their ideas (see Pratt 1992). The zenith of anthropologic theorizing came in the 1950s and 1960s, when structuralists such as Claude Lévi-Strauss (1963, 1967) proposed theories of human cultural relations with physical reality that were cosmological in their implications.

Over its first seven or eight decades, the predominant discourses of the two principal fields of social science that used qualitative and ethnographic methods remained largely aligned in their claims of scientific rigor and objectivity with the "hard" sciences, which included experimental and statistical, quantitative analysis. After a period of social upheaval in Europe and the United States in the late 1960s and 1970s, however, these discourses underwent a period of sustained critique that continues into the present, when a new generation of scholars, along with some of the older generation, began to apply structuralist principles to the analysis of academic culture in the humanities and the social sciences. The product of their combined analyses was not an affirmation of the unity and progressive truth of each discipline's discourses, but rather a demonstration of their organization as a series of conceptual opposites, or binaries, in which the first term in each pair not only opposed but typically oppressed and silenced its defining "other":

| | |
|---|---|
| Objective | Subjective |
| Rational | Emotional |
| Civilized | Savage |

| | |
|---|---|
| Modern | Primitive |
| Scientific | Superstitious |
| Literate | Illiterate |
| Male | Female |
| Light (skinned) | Dark (skinned) |
| Normative (straight) | Deviant (queer) |
| Grand narrative | Anecdote |
| Generalizable | Local |
| Truth | truth |
| Center | Margins |

and so on. The now *post*structural response to this analysis was to bring the marginalized discourses of the right column into the center of academic discourse, by demonstrating that these binaries were not natural but fell apart, or *deconstructed*, under investigations that detailed the homoeroticism inherent in socially and officially very straight groups, for example, or the subjectivity inherent in objective accounts of history, or the lapses of logic and evidence in some theories formerly assumed to be fully scientific in their reasoning. In the service of this project, qualitative and ethnographic research, which had itself always been somewhat marginalized as a practice of the social sciences, was put into service, but not before its traditional alignment with the discursive claims of the center was deconstructed and its inherent contradictions were also exposed.

By the 1980s a series of articles and books challenging the realism of ethnographic narratives (e.g. Brodkey 1987; Clifford and Marcus 1986; Pratt 1992) as misleading in their accuracy and coherence gained prominence within academic discourse. These and later ethnographers (e.g. Foley 1995; Geertz 1983; Lather 1991) championed the value of the local and the small scale and the importance of acknowledging the subjectivity of one's perceptions and interpretations. They altered the purpose of ethnographic and qualitative research, from the building of grand bodies of knowledge to the interruption of claims of normativity and objectivity within social science research.

The case of qualitative and ethnographic approaches within educational research is related and similar, but considerably shorter in its history. Although pioneered in the 1960s and early 1970s in the UK by sociologists studying relations among social class, language practices, and school achievement (e.g. Bernstein 1964; Keddie 1971) and in the USA by linguistic anthropologists studying relations among race and ethnicity, language practices, and school achievement (Labov 1972; Rist 1970), an informal review indicates that qualitative and ethnographic studies were not published routinely in major educational research journals until the late 1980s and early 1990s.

However, once legitimated by publication in major journals, the shift to ethnographic and qualitative research practices, which followed just behind the rise of social theory and disciplinary critique within the humanities and other social sciences, produced a similar shift of seismic proportion within education in what and how issues were investigated and reported. As in the case of social science research, the point of doing educational research was dramatically altered, from contributing to bodies of generalized knowledge to contributing to the subversion of the idea that generalized, objective knowledge existed, and in some cases, to demonstrations of the social injustices perpetrated by claims of objectivity. The introduction of multiple schools of social theory into the discourse—from Soviet-era material psychologists and literary critics to European poststructuralists and the critical theorists of the Frankfurt School to Marxist and neo-Marxist perspectives, provided a vast array of "lenses" and "frameworks" for analysis and writing. New styles of non- or even anti-realist writing were introduced that reveled in their authors' multiple subjectivities, from autoethnography to teacher and action research and other forms of impressionistic and confessional writing. Editors and reviewers were suddenly open to new theories, new methods, and new styles of representation—to almost anything that would break a mold or produce an original insight.

The 1990s were a subversive, creative, and exciting time to be a qualitative, ethnographic educational researcher. As a doctoral student and then researcher in several US universities, I took full advantage of the new freedom within my field of literacy studies. My dissertation and first book, for example, drew on poststructuralism to deconstruct the "natural" distinction between fiction and nonfiction that organizes school libraries in the USA, and documented the ways in which its maintenance ill-served school children (Dressman 1997). I published an impressionistic and partly confessional account of contradictions within the discourses of the Whole Language Movement, which was the dominant approach to early literacy instruction in the USA in the late 1980s and early 1990s (Dressman 1995). Then, after Whole Language was toppled in public policy by a series of experimental studies and reviews of research arguing that the teaching of phonics and phonemic awareness were "scientifically proven" to be more effective, I published a Habermasian (Habermas 1984) analysis demonstrating the internal contradictions and racist assumptions of the "scientific" reasoning that supported this position (Dressman 1999). I was and am fully implicated in the subversion of claims of normative, generalizable knowledge within educational research.

## Consequences

Nearly 20 years after becoming prevalent, little doubt remains that the use of social theory and expanded ways of writing has opened up the discourses of educational research by challenging previous assumptions about the dynamics of race, class, gender, sexuality, and multiple other previously marginalized and denigrated forms of difference. Yet, I will also argue as one of this shift's proponents that it has brought some unexpected consequences as well. For instance, the rise of social theory and of new ways of writing qualitatively did not lead to the demise of quantitative experimental research, to a reduction in the scope of quantitative researchers' claims, or into dialogue with social theory and qualitative research and greater circumspection by the quantitative research community. Instead, at least in the USA, it led to methodological conflict, in which quantitative researchers increasingly codified their practices into dogmatic statements of what was and wasn't "scientific" (e.g. Shavelson and Towne 2002), attacked qualitative research publicly for its lack of systematicity, reliability, and generalizability, and, with the advent of the Bush administration, succeeded in effectively outlawing the consideration of studies that were predominantly qualitative or ethnographic (and that typically made significant use of social theory) from receiving federal funding.

Developments on the part of researchers who use social theory and qualitative, ethnographic methods in their work have been hardly more congenial, however. Over the last decade, discourse and practice have moved from questioning claims of objectivity and generalizability to the overt celebration of subjectivity and localness within research contexts. As an academic and as a reviewer and editor, over time I've noticed an increasing number of manuscripts in which the central focus of the writing is less about the educational issues under investigation and more about the subjective stance of the investigator vi-à-vis the participants, more about the uniqueness of a theoretical framework than about the implications of findings, or more about the uniqueness of a situation than what it reveals about a more general set of conditions—in short, it often seems to me, more about the determination of qualitative researchers to express their own points of view or to stand out in some new and provocative way than to address the pressing social and educational problems of the day. What began as an effort to expand the general parameters of what counted as knowledge about education has evolved, I'll argue, into a way of being, a way of doing identity as much if not more than doing research within the academy and schools, colleges, and faculties of education.

One consequence of these developments, the bifurcation of the educational research community along two largely noncommunicative but intensely engaged binaries, with the consequent diminution of the status and influence of education as a whole, should be fairly obvious. A second, more subtle but no less critical or problematic consequence, and one I hope this book helps to address, is the reduction of social theories' and qualitative, ethnographic research's potential to contribute to the making of general, practical responses to common educational problems in ways that are more than *ad hoc* and more than piecemeal in their effects. This is because as the discourses of qualitative and ethnographic research have become more directly "other" to quantitative research and more actively aligned with subjective ways of knowing and representation, studies have also tended to become more individualized and more self-contained, and therefore have also become less intertextual and less connected to each other and to the possibility of coalescing into bodies of general knowledge or understanding about a phenomenon.

In other words, recent qualitative research studies do not tend to build on each other or "add up" in the same way as quantitative research. For example, quantitative studies of educational phenomena such as phonemic awareness actively reference each other, so that a clear discursive path of ideas and findings from one researcher's study to another is easily identifiable (Dressman 1999). However, in my study of 69 literacy research articles published between 1992 and 2003 (Dressman 2007), it was relatively rare to find qualitative studies on the same topic or even using similar theoretical frameworks referencing and engaging each other's arguments, or to be able to trace the development of ideas or findings through previous research studies. As a consequence, their potential impact on educational practice in general has been largely atomized.

These consequences and others of the shift in focus from the structural to the poststructural and from the lionization of objectivity to the lionization of subjectivity in social research have drawn the attention of other researchers and authors as well. In *The Ethnographic Imagination* (2000), Paul Willis has complained about the poststructural move by which "the sensuous and expressive practices of culture function *like* a language, leaving language queen" (p. 12). By contrast, the ethnographic imagination, he argues in his conclusion, "hopes to render into language that which is formed partly as an escape from language, mentalizing the body again" (p. 125). Willis hopes for an ethnography whose imagination is both collective and personal in its scope and that has an impact for the better on people's social realities—for writing that

> turn(s) a possible local treachery into the means of wider emancipation ...
> This is the 'Ah-ha' effect which in part depends on how far writing

explicates its subject by going through and expanding on the *fullness* of the original by internal reference to wider questions (p. 126)

In *Key Themes in Qualitative Research: Continuities and Change* (2003), Atkinson *et al.* have characterized the turn in ethnographic practice from "old guard" to "avant garde" as both less and more consequential than might be presumed. Each chapter of their book revisits a "classic" ethnographic text and researcher from earlier periods, and finds that these texts present a far more nuanced and conflicted representation of social reality than their later critics typically have given them credit for. They note, for example, Chicago School sociologist Howard Becker's critique of the notion of "value-free" social science, his awareness of the partisan nature of research, and his advocacy for the interests of people over the institutions that controlled their lives. They detail the extent to which early ethnographers self-consciously grappled with issues of intimacy and over-familiarity with people in their field sites, the extent to which they acknowledged the effect of these subjective relationships on their analyses and writing, and the degree to which methodologists have always been aware of the logical contradictions and pitfalls of "classic" analytic procedures, including participant observation, triangulation, and analytic induction. Their revisionist reading of early texts leads them to conclude that there is far greater continuity between old and new ways of doing ethnography than has been acknowledged in the current literature. They also note some serious consequences to the lack of historical awareness within current trends, including the balkanization of ethnography into methodological camps, and, as I have also noted, a focus on personal identity at the expense of social understanding. In conclusion, they argue:

If we are to preserve the essence of the anthropological or sociological imagination, therefore, we need to cultivate still the capacity to *bracket* our own identities and commonsense assumptions, not *only* to celebrate them as personal warrants of knowledge (p. 190, italics in original)

In response, Atkinson *et al.* do not call for a return to "the good old days" of qualitative and ethnographic research, or for a specific program of postreform reform. Rather, they urge current researchers to be more aware of the continuity of problems and issues that qualitative, ethnographic research has faced since its inception, to consider some of the ways that their predecessors dealt with these concerns, and to adopt a more reflexive and self-critical approach toward the subjective turn in recent writing.

Finally, reflexivity is also the signature turn in the methodological writing of theorist Pierre Bourdieu. However, as Bourdieu's co-author, Loïc Wacquant points out in the introduction to *An Invitation to Reflexive Sociology*, Bourdieu's reflexive turn does not lead to subjectivity's full embrace, but rather to a critique of both the "social physics" of objectivism and the "social phenomenology" of subjectivism (Bourdieu and Wacquant 1992): "Far from trying to undermine objectivity, Bourdieu's reflexivity aims at increasing the scope and solidity of social scientific knowledge, a goal which puts it at loggerheads with phenomenological, textual, and other 'postmodern' forms of reflexivity" (pp. 36–37). Bourdieu would have researchers constantly challenge the methodological efficiency and epistemological certainty of social science research, with the goal of producing knowledge that is not absolute in its claims, but that becomes progressively more refined in its capacity to account for all the complexities of social phenomena.

In summary, the three perspectives above either implicitly or explicitly challenge the semiotic relevance, historical accuracy, and methodological utility of abandoning claims of general significance, and of the goal of producing shared knowledge that is objectively validated, within social science research. I join with these authors in their concerns, and in the following sections of this chapter move to a discussion of social theories' potential, in combination with greater rhetorical reflexivity, to claim a place for research framed by social theory in the production of general, empirically validated and practically useful, knowledge about education.

## From generalizable to general educational knowledge

In their embrace of the subjective and critique of objective ways of knowing, the recent practices of qualitative and ethnographic research are fraught with contradictions that, upon closer reading, lead to their deconstruction as well. For example, it has long been an article of faith that the findings of case study research—the detailed analysis of particular individuals or single situations—are not generalizable. Yet, it is also the case that every time an author names the individual or individuals under study as male or female, of a particular race, religion, or ethnicity, of a certain age, or describes the quality of their activity or school performance, that naming immediately invokes a set of general assumptions about what it means to be male or female or Muslim or Catholic or an adolescent or adult or working class or wealthy or bilingual or monolingual. Although it is true that findings from a single case cannot and should not be generalized to an entire population or range of situations, it is equally true that without comparison and contrast to other cases and to generalities about these cases, little meaning could be taken from a single study. Moreover, this is the case regardless of one's research methodology or stylistic approach. A basic semiotic principle is that nothing—art, culture, language, the behavior of groups or individuals—makes sense or can mean anything completely on its own terms. Words—signifiers—are only meaningful because of generally shared signifieds; to use them otherwise in totally subjective ways to produce totally subjective meanings would be to engage in an asocial and unintelligible rant.

A second and perhaps more telling indicator of the search for general meaning within recent qualitative and ethnographic research is many studies' use of social theory as a framework across the multiple stages of a research project. What are social theories, after all, if they are not accounts of general social behavior—that is, not of social behavior within particular cultures or periods of history, but accounts that make claims if not of universality then of generalizability across a broad range of contexts? Language acquisition, as Vygotsky described it, was not referenced solely to the development of young Soviet children, nor were Bakhtin's theories of language and literature meant to describe only the works of Dostoyevsky and other Russian novelists. When Marx described capitalism's dynamics, he did not limit his claims to England or Germany, where he had made his observations. And Foucault's analyses of Enlightenment France were intended as a general indictment of modernity, just as Habermas's Theory of Communicative Action was written as a general description of modernity's unfulfilled but still-achievable promise of social and cultural progress via open public discourse. When educational researchers invoke these theories in support of their own arguments, they mean to connect the localness of their findings and interpretations to broader, more general, and far grander narratives than their own. They are seeking a general meaning for their work, regardless of what they might otherwise claim.

If this is the case, then why isn't social theory more routinely and openly used as a medium whereby the findings of individual studies might be more closely joined together to form general bodies of knowledge about phenomena? I suspect that the answer in part lies in the recent discourses of social science and educational research, in which questions of what constitutes general knowledge have been subsumed within the criteria for statistical generalizability, such as randomized sampling of populations and the use of control groups, as well as by the qualitative and ethnographic research community's renunciation of the objectivity of research claims and its embrace of local meanings and subjective understanding. But it is also due, I suspect, to the ways in which social theories are typically approached by researchers, not as sets of literal propositions that describe social behavior in precise detail, but more as sets of grand ideas that articulate practices and social arrangements researchers would like to see enacted in daily life—that is, as metaphors that give form to researchers' desires for making the world better, i.e. more equitable, more just, and more open to the cultural and social contributions of every member of society. Willis (2000) captures the utility of metaphorical forms of language when he writes:

> None of this is to argue that figurative-metaphoric language is against reason or the carrying or development of thought. Certainly, versions of it may seem to be less suited to analytic reasoning and presentation, but that does not limit figurative language to non-analytic purposes. Metaphoric language is certainly useful to describe things, but it is also and fundamentally useful to think with. It clarifies, or perhaps brings to its only articulation, an abstract idea, or brings out and highlights the abstract quality or essence of something by comparing it to something else, usually concrete, in the world. Where there may be no alternative expression, this is the most condensed thought available (pp. 11–12)

I do not propose to denigrate or deny the power of poetic, metaphorical uses of social theory, but to question whether a field as practically oriented as education is well served by discursive binaries which are so exclusive of each other, so either wildly poetic or prosaically literal in their sense-making that they make no sense to each other, and to ask in conclusion if there is not a way that the poetic could not be less individualistic and more collective and integrative in its imagination.

In response to this last question, I would like to propose a scenario for the use of social theories as media—frameworks—not only for the production of knowledge within individual studies but for the integration of those studies, conducted among diverse populations and locales, into coherent, if sometimes asymmetrical, bodies of general knowledge about a broad range of educational topics, such as classroom discourse, adolescents' use of electronic media, teacher education, or assessment policy. Rick Chavez's fictional research project was organized around one such body of knowledge about social and cultural production and reproduction in secondary schools. That knowledge and its Marxist-based discourses developed over a period of three decades, as researchers across multiple continents entered its conversation with data collected in their localities and analyzed from their perspectives both refined and added dimensionality to the discussion. It was largely unplanned and grew organically from the contributions of multiple researchers over the years.

The scenario I propose, however, is more deliberately coordinated and more synchronous in its activities and discourse. I imagine a group of individual researchers within the same country, region, or even globally, who are interested in similar topics—classroom discourse, adolescents' use of electronic media, teacher education, or assessment policy, for example—and in investigating them through the perspective of a shared social theoretical framework. The individual projects and settings would likely differ in their exact methodologies and feature participants and settings that were diverse but that shared some attributes that were critical to the comparative process, such as age or status (student; teacher; administrator) or setting, i.e. within classrooms or informal educational settings or homes. The individual studies would be conducted within a limited time frame—a year or two years, perhaps—and would be designed, conducted, analyzed, and written up through a process of extensive dialogue and possibly collaboration among researchers, facilitated either through periodic physical meetings or online, web-based interactions. The goal of these projects would be to investigate not only the topic but the fit of the topic with its theoretical framework—to engage social theory in an investigatory way and use it to generate some tentative principles about the dynamics of the topic itself.

As an example, imagine that Rick Chavez did not conduct his research on students' use of videos as a totally independent project, but in conjunction with similar projects in secondary schools in urban, small town, and rural settings on multiple continents and in different cultural regions of the world, from Europe to the Middle East, East Asia, Australia, North America, and Latin America. In this case, Rick might have shared his reading of the literature on social and cultural production and reproduction and multiliteracies with teachers internationally. His reading of these literatures as they applied to his situation might have been challenged in some ways and supported in others by the readings of other teachers in similar, but culturally and politically different, circumstances. He might have continued to meet with Sheila, Edmund, Chris, and his editor (now a coordinator of the project's network of researchers), but he would also have posted his field notes and observations on a web-based discussion forum, and have had a chance to compare the course of his students' progress with that of other classrooms. As he began to analyze and write up his findings, he would have the findings and analyses of others against which to compare his own work, and in his concluding discussion he could discuss relations among his findings and others, just as others could do the same. The result would be a series of studies, each referencing the other, whose sum would provide a multidimensional and theoretically coherent general account of the topic and its dynamics—a perspective against which other researchers in the future might use to frame their work, and add to as well.

The scenario I have described has some precedent in other forms of collective research and publishing within educational research. For example, edited volumes, particularly those whose chapters focus on research framed by a theorist or school of theory (e.g. *Pierre Bourdieu and Literacy Education*, Albright and Luke 2008; *Bakhtinian Perspectives on Language, Literacy, and Learning*, Ball and Freedman 2004), also bring together research conducted in multiple settings but with similar theoretical frameworks. The increase in the publication of handbooks of educational research, which feature encyclopedic reviews of research on a number of topics within a particular field, might also be interpreted as motivated by a desire within educational research for more collective and integrated bodies of knowledge within education. In these two cases, however, the integration of studies is more by proximity (publication within a single volume) or through the efforts of a single author or co-authors, than through the active participation and integrative efforts, of the researchers themselves.

A closer precedent may be the establishment of centers of educational research, such as the Centre for Contemporary Cultural Studies at the University of Birmingham, out of which much of the early research on social and cultural reproduction in education was produced in the 1970s and 1980s, or the centers established in the United States from the 1970s through the 1990s, such as the National Reading Research Center (NRRC) at the University of Illinois at Urbana-Champaign. At NRRC, for example, researchers from around the world came together to investigate the use of schema theory (Anderson *et al.* 1977), a theory of social cognition with conceptual roots in the philosophy of Emmanuel Kant, in explaining processes of reading comprehension. Over the 15 years of its existence, researchers developed a body of knowledge about reading comprehension that has had immense influence on the teaching of reading in schools, and whose comprehensiveness and coherence have not been rivaled since; it stands as a model of the impact that research coordinated within a single theoretical framework can have within educational contexts.

But, centers of the type described here are expensive to fund and are rare, whereas the scenario I have described could be small-scale, web-based in large part, and widespread. Moreover, the scenario I am describing has no personal or geographic "center"; it is a project composed of a number of researchers in different locales who share a topic, a theoretical frame, and a desire to coordinate their knowledge-making activities, and whose leaders emerge from within the group, not from without. It is also truer, in a sense, to the decentered practices and texts of social theory as an organic response to social problems, and truer also in its craftedness, its attention to relations among generalities, particularities, and in its generation of practices that are holistic, that take into account the history and full social context of the educational settings in which they are employed.

I propose, in short, a scenario for educational research that is operational and practical in its goals and outcomes, but poetic in its means and in its language. By "poetic," however, I do not mean research that is slapdash or self-indulgent in its processes or outcomes. As Willis (2000) has noted, figurative-metaphoric language—the poetic—is not against reason, but provides an extraordinary tool for thought. In the hands of great poets, it is language honed-down and refined, meaning condensed, and structured in the most rigorous and rhetorically calculated way possible. The "poetic license" I would give researchers who use social theory would be a license to *drive*—to responsibly and safely take themselves and others to new places—not to make claims that are not substantiated or to rant about the unfairness of the world or one's place in it. This would require a shift in the ways that recent discourses of qualitative and ethnographic research (Denzin and Lincoln 2000; Foley 1995; Goodall 2000; Kamberelis and Dimitriadis 2005) characterize writing, not so much in the turn to experimental, impressionistic and confessional genres, but in the ways that, regardless of genre, arguments about relations among social theory, empirical research, and previous research are developed.

## Summary and conclusion

Throughout this book, I have called for social theory to be used in more interrogative, reflexive ways within educational research and for studies to become more intertextual in their focus—for processes of research and writing that are less defiantly individualistic and more socially and rhetorically focused than recent experiments have tended to be. My desire is for social theories to be integrated into educational research in more powerful ways than they have been in the past, and to be regarded and used as agents that bind multiple studies conducted in diverse contexts into general bodies of knowledge whose collective rhetorical impact on educational policy and practice will be greater than is currently the case outside of academia.

I am less sanguine, however, about the possibility in the foreseeable future for rapprochement with educational researchers who remain steadfastly positivistic—and typically quantitative and experimental—in their approaches. In the United States, at least, the divide between qualitative and quantitative research is too politically motivated, and ideological and epistemological identities are too well established for the complementarity and necessity of both approaches to be fully acknowledged and accepted. A more coordinated and better argued use of social theory within qualitative ethnographic research may bring some respect and attention within educational policy and practice, but it is not likely to "win" any arguments with the other side. Into the future, the narratives of research framed by social theory are likely to continue their function of providing alternative articulations of more just, socially and culturally open, and creative educational environments. To the extent that those articulations are more interrelated and their claims are better reasoned and more fully substantiated, their influence on educational realities is likely to be greater, and the desires of the educational researchers who articulate them are more likely to be realized.

# References

Adams, M. J. (1990) *Beginning to Read: Thinking and Learning about Print*, Cambridge, MA: MIT Press.

Albright, J. and Luke, A. (eds) (2008) *Pierre Bourdieu and Literacy Education*, New York: Routledge.

Althusser, L. (1971) *Lenin and Philosophy, and Other Essays,* trans. B. Brewster, London: New Left Books.

Anderson, R. C., Reynolds, R. E., Schallert, D. L. and Goetz, E. T. (1977) "Frameworks for comprehending discourse," *American Educational Research Journal,* 14: 367-381.

Appadurai, A. (1996) *Modernity at Large: Cultural Dimensions of Globalization*, Minneapolis: University of Minnesota Press.

Ashley, H. (2001) "Playing the game: Proficient working-class student writers' second voices," *Research in the Teaching of English*, 35: 493-524.

Atkinson, P., Coffey, A. and Delamont, S. (2003) *Key Themes in Qualitative Research: Continuities and Change,* Lanham: AltaMira Press.

Austin, J. L. (1975) *How to Do Things with Words,* Cambridge, MA: Harvard University Press.

Bakhtin, M. (1973) *Problems of Dostoevsky's Politics,* trans. R. W. Rostel, Ann Arbor: Ardis.

Bakhtin, M. M. (1981) *The Dialogic Imagination: Four Essays by M. M. Bakhtin*, M. Holquist (ed.) trans. C. Emerson and M. Holquist, Austin: University of Texas Press.

Ball, A. F. and Freedman, S. W. (eds) (2004) *Bakhtinian Perspectives on Language, Literacy, and Learning,* Cambridge, UK: Cambridge University Press.

Bandura, A. (1986) *Social Foundations of Thought and Action: A Social Cognitive Theory,* Englewood Cliffs: Prentice Hall.

Baudrillard, J. (1988) *Jean Baudrillard: Selected Writings,* M. Poster (ed.) Stanford: Stanford University Press.

Bauer, H. H. (1994) *Scientific Literacy and the Myth of the Scientific Method*, Champaign: University of Illinois Press.

Bell, D. A. (2004) *Race, Racism, and American Law*, 4th edn, Gaithersburg: Aspen Law and Business.

Bernstein, B. (1964) "Elaborated and restricted codes: Their social origins and some consequences," *American Anthropologist,* 66: 55-69.

Best, S. and Kellner, D. (1991) *Postmodern Theory: Critical Interrogations*, New York: Guilford Press.

Best, S. and Kellner, D. (1997) *The Postmodern Turn*, New York: Guilford Press.

Bourdieu, P. (1984) *Distinction: A Social Critique of the Judgment of Taste*, Cambridge, MA: Harvard University Press.

Bourdieu, P. (1989) "Social space and symbolic power," *Sociological Theory*, 7: 14-25.

Bourdieu, P. (1990) *The Logic of Practice*, trans. R. Nice, Stanford: Stanford University Press.

Bourdieu, P. and Passeron, J. C. (1977) *Reproduction in Education, Society, and Culture*, London: Sage.

Bourdieu, P. and Wacquant, L. (1992) *An Invitation to Reflexive Sociology*, Chicago: University of Chicago Press.

Bowles, S. and Gintis, H. (1976) *Schooling in Capitalist America: Educational Reform and the Contradictions of Economic Life*, New York: Basic Books.

Brenner, W. H. (1999) *Wittgenstein's Philosophical Investigations*, Albany: State University of New York Press.

Brodkey, L. (1987) *Academic Writing as Social Practice*, Philadelphia: Temple University Press.

Brown, J. S., Collins, A. and Duguid, S. (1989) "Situated cognition and the culture of learning," *Educational Researcher*, 18(1): 32-42.

Butler, J. (1990) *Gender Trouble: Feminism and the Subversion of Identity*, New York: Routledge.

Butler, J. (1993) *Bodies that Matter: On the Discursive Limits of Sex*, London: Routledge.

Callahan, R. E. (1962) *Education and the Cult of Efficiency: A Study of the Social Forces that Have Shaped the Administration of the Public Schools*, Chicago: University of Chicago Press.

Campbell, J. (1968) *The Hero with a Thousand Faces*, Princeton: Princeton University Press.

Carspecken, P. F. (1996) *Critical Ethnography in Educational Research: A Theoretical and Practical Guide*, New York: Routledge.

Cazden, C. B. (2001) *Classroom Discourse: The Language of Teaching and Learning*, 2nd edn, Portsmouth, NH: Heinemann.

Clifford, J. and Marcus, G. E. (eds) (1986) *Writing Culture: The Poetics and Politics of Ethnography*, Berkeley: University of California Press.

Cochran-Smith, M. and Lytle, S. L. (eds) (1992) *Inside/Outside: Teacher Research and Knowledge*, New York: Teachers College Press.

Connell, R. W. (1987) *Gender and Power*, Stanford: Stanford University Press.

Cook-Sather, A. (2006) "Newly betwixt and between: Revising liminality in the context of a teacher preparation program," *Anthropology and Education Quarterly*, 37: 110-127.

Darwin, C. (1939) *The Origin of Species*, London: J. M. Dent and Sons.

Deci, E. L. and Ryan, R. M. (1985) *Intrinsic Motivation and Self-Determination in Human Behavior*, New York: Plenum.

Deleuze, G. and Guattari, F. (1987) *A Thousand Plateaus: Capitalism and Schizophrenia*, trans. B. Massumi, Minneapolis: University of Minnesota Press.

Denzin, N. (1996) *Interpretive Ethnography: Ethnographic Practices for the 21st Century*, Thousand Oaks: Sage.

Denzin, N. and Lincoln, Y. (2000) *Handbook of Qualitative Research*, Thousand Oaks: Sage.

Derrida, J. (1976) *Of Grammatology*, trans. G. C. Spivak, Baltimore: Johns Hopkins University Press.

Dewey, J. (1919) *Democracy and Education*, New York: Macmillan.

Dewey, J. and Bentley, A. (1949) *Knowing and the Known*, Boston: Beacon Press.

Dolby, N. and Dimitriadis, G. (2004) *Learning to Labor in New Times*, New York: RoutledgeFalmer.

Dressman, M. (1993) "Lionizing lone wolves: The cultural romantics of literacy workshops," *Curriculum Inquiry,* 23: 245-263.

Dressman, M. (1995) "Under the umbrella: Resisting the reign of rationalized educational reform," *Journal of Curriculum Studies,* 27: 231-244.

Dressman, M. (1997) *Literacy in the Library: Negotiating the Spaces between Order and Desire,* Westport, CT: Bergin and Garvey.

Dressman, M. (1998) "Confessions of a methods fetishist; or, the cultural politics of reflective non-engagement," in R. Chavez and J. O'Donnell (eds) *Speaking the Unpleasant: The Politics of Non-Engagement in the Multicultural Education Terrain,* Albany: State University of New York Press.

Dressman, M. (1999) "On the use and misuse of research evidence: Decoding two states' reading initiatives," *Reading Research Quarterly,* 34: 258-285.

Dressman, M. (2004) "Dewey and Bakhtin in dialogue: From Rosenblatt to a pedagogy of literature as social, aesthetic practice," in A. Ball and S. Freedman (eds) *Bakhtinian Perspectives on Language, Literacy, and Learning,* Cambridge, UK: Cambridge University Press.

Dressman, M. (2007) "Theoretically framed: Argument and desire in the production of general knowledge about literacy," *Reading Research Quarterly,* 42: 332-363.

Dressman, M. and Webster, J. P. (2001) "Retracing Rosenblatt: A textual archaeology," *Research in the Teaching of English,* 36: 110-145.

Elbow, P. (1973) *Writing without Teachers,* New York: Oxford University Press.

Everhart, R. B. (1983) *Reading, Writing, and Resistance: Adolescents and Labor in a Junior High School,* Boston: Routledge and Kegan Paul.

Fairclough, N. (1995) *Critical Discourse Analysis: The Critical Study of Language,* London: Longman.

Fairclough, N. (2003) *Analysing Discourse: Textual Analysis for Social Research,* London: Routledge.

Feyerabend, P. (1993) *Against Method,* New York: Verso.

Fiske, J. (1987) *Television Culture,* New York: Routledge.

Fiske, J. (1989) *Reading the Popular,* Cambridge, MA: Unwin Hyman.

Foley, D. E. (1990) *Learning Capitalist Culture: Deep in the Heart of Tejas,* Philadelphia: University of Pennsylvania Press.

Foley, D. E. (1995) *The Heartland Chronicles,* Philadelphia: University of Pennsylvania Press.

Foucault, M. (1977) *Discipline and Punish: The Birth of the Prison,* trans. A. Sheridan, New York: Vintage.

Foucault, M. (1980) *Power/Knowledge: Selected Interviews and Other Writings, 1972-1977,* trans. C. Gordon (ed.), Sussex: Harvester.

Foucault, M. (1986) "Of other spaces," trans. J. Miskowiec, *Diacritics,* 16: 22-27.

Foucault, M. (1994) *The Order of Things: An Archaeology of the Human Sciences,* New York: Vintage.

Freire, P. (1970) *Pedagogy of the Oppressed,* trans. M. B. Ramos, New York: Herder and Herder.

Gadamer, H. G. (1994) *Truth and Method,* New York: Continuum.

Gee, J. (2005) *An Introduction to Discourse Analysis: Theory and Method,* 2nd edn, New York: Routledge.

Gee, J. (2007) *Social Linguistics and Literacies: Ideology in Discourses*, 3$^{rd}$ edn, London: Taylor and Francis.

Geertz, C. (1983) *Local Knowledge: Further Essays in Interpretive Anthropology*, New York: Basic Books.

Geertz, C. (2000) *The Interpretation of Cultures: Selected Essays*, New York: Basic Books.

Glaser, B. and Strauss, A. (1967) *The Discovery of Grounded Theory: Strategies for Qualitative Research,* Chicago: Aldine.

Goodall, H. I. (2000) *Writing the New Ethnography*, Lanham: AltaMira.

Gould, S. J. (1996) *The Mismeasure of Man*, New York: Norton.

Gramsci, A. (1988) *An Antonio Gramsci Reader: Selected Writings, 1916-1935*, D. Forgacs (ed.), New York: Schocken Books.

Habermas, J. (1984) *The Theory of Communicative Action, Vol. I: Reason and the Rationalization of Society*, Boston: Beacon Press.

Holquist, M. (2002) *Dialogism: Bakhtin and His World*, London: Routledge.

Iser, W. (1979) *The Implied Reader: Patterns of Communication in Prose Fiction from Bunyan to Beckett*, Baltimore: Johns Hopkins University Press.

Ito, M. (2006) "Engineering play: Children's software and the cultural politics of edutainment," *Discourse: Studies in the Cultural Politics of Education,* 27: 149-160.

Jameson, F. (1975) *The Prison-House of Language*, Princeton: Princeton University Press.

Jauss, H. R. (1982) *Toward an Aesthetic of Reception*, Minneapolis: University of Minnesota Press.

Jenkins, R. (2002) *Pierre Bourdieu*, London: Routledge.

Jung, C. (1968) *Man and His Symbols*, New York: Dell.

Kaartinen, S. and Kumpulainen, K. (2001) "Negotiating meaning in science classroom communities: Cases across age levels," *Journal of Classroom Interaction*, 36: 4-16.

Kamberelis, G. and Dimitriadis, G. (2005) *On Qualitative Inquiry: Approaches to Language and Literacy Research*, New York: Teachers College Press.

Keddie, N. (1971) "Classroom knowledge," in M. Young (ed.), *Knowledge and Control*, London: Collier-Macmillan.

Knobel, M., and Lankshear, C. (2002) "Cut, paste, and publish: The production and consumption of zines," In D. E. Alvermann (ed.), *Adolescents and Literacies in a Digital World*, New York: Peter Lang.

Kolakowski, L. and Falla, P. S. (2005) *Main Currents of Marxism: The Founders, the Golden Age, the Breakdown,* New York: W. W. Norton and Company.

Kress, G., and van Leeuwen, T. (2006) *Reading Images: The Grammar of Visual Design*, New York: Routledge.

Kuhn, T. (1996) *The Structure of Scientific Revolutions*, Chicago: University of Chicago Press.

Labov, W. (1972) *Language in the Inner City: Studies in the Black English Vernacular,* Philadelphia: University of Pennsylvania Press.

Ladson-Billings, G. J. (1995) "Toward a critical race theory of education," *Teachers College Record,* 97: 47-68.

Lather, P. A. (1991) *Getting Smart: Feminist Research and Pedagogy with/in the Postmodern,* New York: Routledge.

Latour, B. (2005) *Reassembling the Social: An Introduction to Actor-Network Theory*, Oxford: Oxford University Press.

Lave, J., and Wenger, E. (1991) *Situated Learning: Legitimate Peripheral Participation*, New York: Cambridge University Press.

Lemke, J. "New media and new learning communities: Critical, creative, and independent," paper presented at National Council of Teachers of English Assembly for Research, Nashville, TN, February, 2007.

Lensmire, T. J. (2000) *Powerful Writing, Responsible Teaching*, New York: Teachers College Press.

Leseman, P. P. M. and De Jong, P. F. (1998) "Home literacy: Opportunity, instruction, cooperation and social-emotional quality predicting early reading achievement," *Reading Research Quarterly*, 33: 294-318.

Levinson, B., Foley, D. E. and Holland, D. C. (1996) *The Cultural Production of the Educated Person: Critical Ethnographies of Schooling and Local Practice*, Albany: State University of New York Press.

Lévi-Strauss, C. (1963) *Structural Anthropology*, trans. C. Jacobson and B. G. Schoepf, New York: Basic Books.

Lévi-Strauss, C. (1967) *Tristes Tropiques*, trans. J. Russell, New York: Atheneum.

Lincoln, Y. S. and Guba, E. G. (1985) *Naturalistic Inquiry*, Newbury Park: Sage.

Longino, H. E. (1990) *Science as Social Knowledge: Values and Objectivity in Scientific Inquiry*, Princeton: Princeton University Press.

Macey, D. (1993) *The Lives of Michel Foucault: A Biography*, New York: Pantheon.

McLaren, P. (1986) *Schooling as a Ritual Performance: Towards a Political Economy of Educational Symbols and Gestures*, London: Routledge and Kegan Paul.

McLellan, D. (ed.) (1988) *Marxism: Essential Writings*, Oxford: Oxford University Press.

MacLeod, Jay (1987) *Ain't No Makin' It: Leveled Aspirations in a Low-Income Neighborhood*, Boulder: Westview Press.

McRobbie, A. (1991) *Feminism and Youth Culture: From Jackie to Just Seventeen*, Boston: Unwin Hyman.

Monk, R. (1990) *Ludwig Wittgenstein: The Duty of Genius*, New York: Penguin.

Nietzsche, F. W. (1955) *Beyond Good and Evil*, trans. M. Cowan, Chicago: Gateway Editions.

Nietzsche, F. W. (2006) *Thus Spoke Zarathustra: A Book for All and None*, trans. A. Del Caro, A. Del Caro and R. B. Pippin (eds), Cambridge, UK: Cambridge University Press.

Norris, C. (2002) *Deconstruction: Theory and Practice*, London: Routledge.

Popkewitz, T. S. (1998) "Dewey, Vygotsky, and the social administration of the individual: Constructivist pedagogy as systems of ideas in historical spaces," *American Educational Research Journal*, 35: 535-570.

Porat, D. A. (2006) "Who fired first? Students' construction of meaning from one textbook account of the Israeli-Arab conflict," *Curriculum Inquiry*, 36: 251-271.

Pratt, M. L. (1992) *Imperial Eyes: Travel Writing and Transculturation*, New York: Routledge.

Prior, P. (1995) "Tracing authoritative and internally persuasive discourses: A case study of response, revision, and disciplinary enculturation," *Research in the Teaching of English*, 29: 288-325.

Propp, V. (1968) *Morphology of the Folktale*, 2nd edn, trans. L. Scott, Austin: University of Texas Press.

Renold, E. (2006) "'They won't let us play ... unless you're going out with one of them': Girls, boys and Butler's 'heterosexual matrix' in the primary years," *British Journal of Sociology of Education*, 27: 489-509.

Rist, R. (1970) "Student social class and teacher expectations," *Harvard Educational Review*, 40: 411-451.

Rosenblatt, L. (1978) *The Reader, the Text, the Poem: The Transactional Theory of the Literary Work*, Carbondale: Southern Illinois University Press.

Rowe, D. W. and Leander, K. M. (2006) "Mapping literacy spaces in motion: A rhizomatic analysis of a classroom literacy performance," *Reading Research Quarterly,* 41: 428-460.

Rundle, B. (1990) *Wittgenstein and Contemporary Philosophy of Language,* Cambridge, MA: Blackwell.

Saïd, E. (1978) *Orientalism*, New York: Pantheon.

Saïd, E. (1993) *Culture and Imperialism*, New York: Random House.

Saussure, F. (1966) *Course in General Linguistics*, trans. A. Sechehaye, C. Bally (ed.), New York: McGraw-Hill.

Schwandt, T. (2002) *Evaluation Practice Reconsidered*, New York: Peter Lang.

Searle, J. (1969) *Speech Acts*, Cambridge, UK: Cambridge University Press.

Shapin, S. (1996) *The Scientific Revolution*, Chicago: University of Chicago Press.

Shavelson, R. J., and Towne, L. (eds) (2002) *Scientific Research in Education*, Washington: National Academy Press.

Sheehy, M. (2002) "Illuminating constructivism: Structure, discourse, and subjectivity in a middle-school classroom," *Reading Research Quarterly,* 37: 278-308.

Smart, B. (2002) *Michel Foucault*, London: Routledge.

Spencer, H. (1894) *Aphorisms from the Writings of Herbert Spencer*, J. R. Gingell (ed.), New York: D. Appleton and Co.

Stake, R. E. (1995) *The Art of Case Study Research*, Thousand Oaks: Sage.

Stanovich, K. E. (1986) "Matthew effects in reading: Some consequences of individual differences in the acquisition of literacy," *Reading Research Quarterly,* 21: 360-406.

Talbani, A. (1996) "Pedagogy, power, and discourse: Transformation of Islamic education," *Comparative Education Review,* 40: 66-82.

Thompson, K. (ed.) (1985) *Readings from Emile Durkheim,* New York: Routledge.

Toulmin, S. E. (1958) *The Uses of Argument,* Cambridge, UK: Cambridge University Press.

Toulmin, S. E. (1990) *Cosmopolis: The Hidden Agenda of Modernity*, Chicago: University of Chicago Press.

Toulmin, S. E. (2001) *Return to Reason*, Cambridge, MA: Harvard University Press.

Turner, V. (1969) *The Ritual Process: Structure and Anti-Structure*, Ithaca: Cornell University Press.

Turner, V. (1974) *Dramas, Fields, and Metaphors: Symbolic Action in Human Society*, Ithaca: Cornell University Press.

Turner, V. (1981) "Social dramas and stories about them," in W. J. T. Mitchell (ed.), *On Narrative* (pp. 137-164), Chicago: University of Chicago Press.

Van Maanen, J. (1988) *Tales of the Field: On Writing Ethnography*, Chicago: University of Chicago Press.

Vaughan, M., and Mark-Lawson, J. (1986) "The downgrading of the humanities in French and English secondary education," *Comparative Education,* 22: 133-147.

Vygotsky, L. S. (1978) *Mind in Society,* M. Cole (ed.), Cambridge, MA: Harvard University Press.

Vygotsky, L. S. (1986) *Thought and Language*, rev. edn, A. Kozulin (ed.), Cambridge, MA: MIT Press.

Wallis, C., Steptoe, S. and Miranda, C. A. (2006) "How to bring our schools out of the 20$^{th}$ century," *Time*, 168(25): 50-56.

Weber, M. (1962) *Basic Concepts in Sociology,* trans. H. P. Secher, New York: Philosophical Library.

Weis, L. (1990) *Working Class without Work: High School Students in a De-Industrializing Economy*, New York: Routledge.

Wertsch, J. V. (1985) *Vygotsky and the Social Formation of Mind*, Cambridge, MA: Harvard University Press.

Wertsch, J. V. (2002) *Voices of Collective Remembering*, Cambridge, UK: Cambridge University Press.

Willis, P. E. (1977) *Learning to Labour: How Working Class Kids Get Working Class Jobs*, Farnborough: Saxon House.

Willis, P. E. (2000) *The Ethnographic Imagination*, Cambridge, UK: Polity.

Wittgenstein, L. (1922) *Tractatus Logico-Philosophicus*, London: Kegan Paul.

Wittgenstein, L. (1953) *Philosophical Investigations*, Oxford: Blackwell.

Worsley, P. (2002) *Marx and Marxism*, London: Routledge.

Young, J. P. (2000) "Boy Talk: critical literacy and masculinities," *Reading Research Quarterly,* 35: 312-337.

# Index